Colorful Food for the Soul

Recipes That Nourish the Body and Engage the Spirit

Lucinda Freeman

Also by Lucinda Freeman:
Historic Houston: How to See It

LifeRich Publishing is a registered trademark of The Reader's Digest Association, Inc.

LifeRich Publishing books may be ordered through booksellers or by contacting:

LifeRich Publishing
1663 Liberty Drive
Bloomington, IN 47403
www.liferichpublishing.com
1 (888) 238-8637

ISBN: 978-1-4897-0262-3 (sc)
ISBN: 978-1-4897-0261-6 (hc)
ISBN: 978-1-4897-0263-0 (e)

Library of Congress Control Number: 2014914774

Printed in the United States of America.

LifeRich Publishing rev. date: 10/24/2014

To my "foodie" friends and family who have been supportive in so many ways.

Many thanks to these enthusiastic recipe testers: Amy Stevens, Charlsie Neathery, Crystal Young, Helene Henson, Henrietta Freeman, Nina Freeman, Jane Ista, Julie Biggerstaff, Lisa Martinson, Melinda McAlister, Nicole Wyman, Phyllis Camara, and Rebecca Reyna. Your reviews were much appreciated! And to my mother, Marion, and sister, Caroline; to my nutritionist friend Sue Thompson and her mother, Bea, for their honest feedback, counsel, and encouragement.

To the staff at Martha's Bloomers and Café M. Bloomers in Navasota, Texas, who readily offered me the opportunity to conduct cooking classes at their tearoom, despite my having no formal references in the culinary world. Thank you Joyce Holcomb and Bonnie Larsen for taking a risk on me, and thank you, Cynthie Thomas of Yellow Rose Marketing, for your lovely recipe booklets and decorations for the classes—not to mention being my sous chef!

Contents

Preface

I decided to write this book because I get great enjoyment from cooking, and I'd like to spread the word about how easy, fun, and satisfying it can be! I've found that cooking can be a great way to express your individual creativity, and unlike being a painter or musician, you can eat your work! Speaking of painting, I have discovered that by eating the whole palette of color, you can nourish the body as well as the soul. Fruits and veggies star in this way of eating. Many thanks to the book *The Color Code* for getting me started down that path.

My enthusiasm led to more than six hundred recipes! I decided there is a fine line between enthusiasm and exhaustion, and I kept only my favorites. In part, I made decisions by the "eyebrow" test. I realized that when I tasted my favorite recipes, I raised my eyebrows inadvertently—my personal "yum" indicator.

My wish is to provide you a template of recipes that are colorful, fun, and flexible. I hope you will become engaged in the adventure of cooking, add your own stamp of creativity to the process, and find true yumminess!

Introduction

Cooking with color is an excellent way to unleash your creativity and amp up your nutrition intake. To make your experience in using this book more satisfying, I emphasize straightforward recipes that engage multiple senses. On a rough day, there is nothing more satisfying than slapping around some bread dough, watching it rise, smelling it bake, and tasting that warm, yeasty goodness right out of the oven!

Your mother was right: you should eat your vegetables. And many of us should eat a lot more of them. To me, this is intimidating. So I include ideas for how to eat your vegetables throughout the day, including snack time. Why not whip up delicious red or green pesto: simply throw a few colorful ingredients in a food processor, whirl a few times, then presto! You've got pesto to spread on a cracker, for a midday snack, or—even better—to enjoy at cocktail time, with a glass of wine.

While we're told to eat more veggies, we're also told to be mindful of calories. Although this is not a low-calorie cookbook, I adapt recipes to conserve calories where feasible, while preserving the spirit and flavor of the dish. For instance, I offer an option to use light butter or light mayonnaise in some recipes, and buttermilk instead of cream in some creamy soups. I hope you will agree that eating attractive, colorful food can help you savor the food, and you may find that you eat more mindfully.

I do my best to keep things as simple as possible. I incorporate ingredients that are easy to find, or I offer substitutes. For flexibility, I offer multiple ways to make and use recipes. A basic hollandaise can be morphed into béarnaise or aioli, for instance, and can accompany many dishes, from eggs benedict to steamed veggies to steak. Pomegranate pepper preserves can be served over Brie, or with ham and cheese sandwiches, pork, beef, or fish. They also make a unique hostess gift.

Are you the thrifty type? Hate to throw away food, especially aging produce? Want to save space in your fridge? I've got you covered. Look for recipes like these: blueberry sauce, summer tomato jam, quick cucumber salad, chimichurri sauce, creamed spinach, broccoli or kale pesto, or roasted cauliflower puree.

Last but not least, I've included some favorite recipes from my neck of the woods, Texas. Culturally speaking, we're located where Old South, Southwest, and Tex-Mex cuisines converge. In my chapter "Favorites from the South and Southwest," check out ideas like seafood gumbo, fried green tomatoes, and Southwestern pulled pork. For dessert, try one of several bread puddings, or *Tres Leches* cake.

My overarching goal is to inspire you to cook more—and add your own stamp of creativity to recipes—so that the experience of creating tasty and nutritious food becomes uniquely yours. In some recipes, you'll see ideas submitted by friends of mine who were recipe testers for this book, offering their own ideas. What fun!

Throughout the book you will find these icons that will enhance your experience:

 here's one idea; make it your own!

 historical or cultural factoid

 calorie-wise

 nutrient-rich

 time-saving

By the way: being creative is a continuous process of discovery, so I've established a website that highlights new experiments and efforts, such as cooking classes. Click on colorfulfoodforthesoul.com. And follow me on twitter @colorfoodsoul.

Enjoy the adventure! Bon voyage, and bon appetit!

Appetizers

Dried Apricots with Blue Cheese and Walnuts

6 appetizer servings

Dried apricots are a good source of Vitamin A, potassium, and fiber. Walnuts are high in Omega 3's, which are good for the brain and the heart.

Ingredients

1 dozen dried apricots

4 oz. cream cheese, softened

2–3 oz. blue cheese crumbles—to taste

¼ cup chopped walnuts

2–3 tbsp. honey

12 walnut halves, toasted, for topping

Directions

In an oven or toaster oven, toast walnut halves and pieces at 325 degrees for 5–6 minutes.

In medium bowl, combine cream cheese, blue cheese, and chopped walnuts. Spread about a teaspoonful onto apricots. Top with a dollop of honey, then a walnut half. If desired, drizzle with additional honey.

Build Your Own Hummus

About 1½ cups

Hummus has become so popular that farmers are taking notice. US chickpea production is up 50 percent year over year as of April 2013. Maybe that's because chickpeas are a good, ready source of iron and fiber. I like to use almond butter instead of tahini since I have more uses for it.

Ingredients
Basic Recipe

1 can chickpeas (garbanzo beans), drained, reserving ¼ cup liquid

Juice of 1 lemon: about 2 tbsp.

2 tbsp. sesame tahini (or a nut butter such as almond butter)

5 cloves garlic

2–3 tbsp. olive oil to taste

Salt and pepper to taste

Directions

Mix all in a food processor until combined well. Check for taste and texture.

Add one or more optional items to taste:

¼ cup minced parsley or cilantro, or 2 tsp. coriander/cilantro chutney, separate recipe

1 roasted red bell pepper from a jar

2 tbsp. Kalamata olives

1 shallot, quartered

½ can drained and rinsed artichoke hearts

½ tsp. smoked paprika

Up to ½ cup toasted nuts, such as pine nuts, pistachios, or walnuts

1 or 2 dashes hot sauce

Serve with crudités, pita chips, or your favorite crackers. For an unusual flavor combination: *goat cheese*. To basic recipe, add ¼ cup roasted/salted pistachios or other nuts, and 2 oz. goat cheese, plus optional items if desired.

Variation: White Bean Hummus

Follow directions for chickpea hummus, using basic ingredients, and adding about ¼ cup chopped artichoke hearts, 2 chopped green onions, ¼ cup chopped parsley, and ¼ cup toasted nuts. Add additional items to taste.

Pumpkin Hummus (for Fall):

Add ½ cup pure pumpkin, from a can, to basic recipe (more to taste). Add 1 tsp. dried thyme. Increase nut butter to 3 tbsp. Add dash of smoked paprika, white or black pepper if desired. Decorate with pepitas (pumpkin seeds).

Mini Cheese Tortas with Red and Green Pestos
Makes 8–12 mini tortas

Both red and green pestos are packed with nutrients!

Ingredients

1 6–8 oz. log Brie cheese—or make round discs from another mild soft cheese
½ cup prepared green pesto—store bought, or see separate recipe
½ cup prepared roasted red bell pepper pesto, separate recipe

Optional: ¼ cup prepared Kalamata olive tapenade, separate recipe

Topping: ⅓ cup roasted pine nuts or chopped roasted pistachios

Directions

Line a muffin tin with paper liners. Slice cheese thinly. Place a slice in muffin liner. Spread with about 1 tsp. red pesto. Repeat, using green pesto. Place a third slice of cheese on top, and top with a small dollop of one of the pestos or the tapenade. Sprinkle with nuts. Lift out the liners; place on individual plates or serving plate. Serve with crackers.

Wild Mushroom Pasta Sauce and Tart Filling

Makes about 2 cups of sauce

Mushrooms are rich in vitamins and minerals. They provide significant amounts of niacin, riboflavin, copper, selenium, potassium, and vitamin D. They have also been shown to fight breast cancer. Citrus zests are high in fiber and flavonoids, which fight cancer and diabetes. They also lower cholesterol.

Variations

Serve over linguine and top with grated Parmesan. For tarts, fill cooked tart shells with warm filling.

Ingredients

1 oz. dried mushrooms, such as Porcini: about 1 cup, loosely packed

½ cup broth from hydrating dried mushrooms

2 tbsp. unsalted butter—regular or light

⅓ cup finely chopped shallots

8 oz. fresh mushrooms of your choice, sliced

3 cloves garlic, minced

½ tsp. kosher salt and about ½ tsp. freshly ground pepper

3 tbsp. dry sherry or other dry white wine

2 tbsp. plain Greek yogurt

¼ cup heavy cream

1 tsp. dried thyme or tarragon

1 tbsp. truffle oil or olive oil; truffle oil is highly recommended for its unique flavor

Juice and zest of 1 lemon (about 2 tsp. lemon zest and 2 tbsp. lemon juice)

2 tsp. Worcestershire sauce

4 oz. grated Fontina or Parmesan cheese, or a combination of the two

Optional: dash hot sauce

For tarts, use baked tart shells.

Directions

Pour 1 cup boiling water over dried mushrooms. Allow to stand for 30 minutes. Drain through a strainer using a paper towel, coffee filter, or cheesecloth, reserving liquid. Rinse mushrooms to remove any debris. You should have about ½ cup liquid. Coarsely chop mushrooms. Place the liquid in a small saucepan; simmer while you prepare remaining mixture. Broth should reduce by half.

Melt butter in a large saucepan over medium heat. Add shallots; cook until softened, about 2 minutes. Add fresh mushrooms, garlic, salt, and pepper; cook until mushrooms are softened and golden brown, 4 to 6 minutes. Add rehydrated mushrooms and wine, bring to a boil, and cook until wine is mostly absorbed, about 3 minutes. Add yogurt, cream, and tarragon or thyme; cook, stirring until most liquid is absorbed, about 3 minutes.

Stir reduced broth into mushroom mixture, along with lemon juice, zest, Worcestershire sauce, and truffle oil. Simmer for about 5 minutes over medium-low heat. Stir in grated cheese until melted, reserving about ½ cup for garnish.

Pecan Tart Shells and Pecan-Cheese Wafers

Makes about 2 cups of dough or about 3 dozen wafers

Serving Ideas

Fill baked tart shells with a sweet citrus curd, see separate recipe. Or, for a savory filling, fill shells with goat cheese, mascarpone, or cream cheese. Top with pesto or hot pepper preserves if desired; see separate recipes for apricot-pepper and pomegranate-pepper preserves.

Ingredients

1 cup pecan pieces, toasted
1 cup mascarpone cheese, softened
4 tbsp. unsalted butter, softened and cut into
    several pieces
1½ cups all-purpose flour

1 tsp. kosher salt
For cheese wafers, use 2 cups finely grated
    cheddar, Parmesan, or Swiss cheese
Optional: cayenne or paprika pepper, for dusting
    wafers

Directions

Using a food processor, pulse pecan pieces until they are very fine. Add mascarpone and butter; pulse until well combined. Add flour and salt; pulse until mixture comes together, wiping down sides and bottom of bowl.

For mini-tart shells, roll into teaspoon-sized balls. Press into muffin tin. Bake on upper oven rack at 350 degrees for about 20 minutes, until sides are starting to brown and bottoms look cooked.

For cheese-filled tarts, bake halfway, fill with cheese, then finish baking.

For pecan-cheese wafers, add cheese to dough; mix well. Add a generous dose of black pepper if you like. Roll into rounded teaspoon-size balls, then press onto a foil- or parchment-lined cookie sheet, using tines of a fork. Flatten well, so that they'll cook through. Sprinkle with cayenne or paprika if desired. Bake on top oven rack until done, about 25 minutes. Bottoms should be nicely browned and tops beginning to brown.

Spanakopita Pinwheels or Tarts

About 1½ cups filling; easily doubled

In addition to its well-known iron content, spinach provides good amounts of beta-carotene, potassium, vitamins C and K, and folate (for heart health). Citrus zests are high in fiber and flavonoids, which fight cancer and diabetes, and lower cholesterol.

Filling can be refrigerated up to 24 hours before using.

Ingredients

1 sheet puff pastry, thawed, for pinwheels (or use prepared pie dough)

½ cup minced red onion

1 tbsp. olive oil

6 oz. baby spinach (coarsely chopped) plus 2 tbsp. water for cooking

2 oz. Feta cheese, crumbled

¼ cup ricotta cheese

1 large egg, beaten (eliminate for pinwheels)   Salt and pepper to taste (remember, Feta is salty)
2 tsp. lemon zest

Directions

In a heavy saucepan, sauté onion in oil over medium heat until soft, 4–5 minutes, stirring often. Add spinach and water. Stir until spinach is cooked and reduced, and little to no liquid is present, several minutes. Remove from heat; stir in cheeses until well combined. Add egg, lemon zest, salt, and pepper. Mix well, making sure no large lumps exist. Refrigerate up to 24 hours if desired.

For Pinwheels

Roll out pastry to a 12-inch square. Spread cooled cheese/spinach mixture over the square. Roll up and refrigerate at least one hour, to firm up. Preheat oven to 375 degrees. Cut the log in half to make it easier to slice. Slice each remaining log into about 12 slices, about ¼ inch thick. Put on cookie sheets lined with parchment paper. Bake 15–18 minutes, until starting to brown.

For Tarts

Press dough into muffin liners that have been coated with nonstick spray. Fill; bake tarts 18–22 minutes, until filling is firm and crust is beginning to brown. Cool 10 minutes before removing from tin.

Soups

Crockpot Ham and Navy Bean Soup

6–8 servings

Navy beans are so named because they were a staple food of the US Navy in the early twentieth century. They are interchangeable with great northern or cannellini beans. Navy beans contain many minerals, including calcium, iron, magnesium, and potassium. They are a good source of fiber and provide heart benefits. Carrots, celery, onion, and tomatoes amp up the nutrition.

Ingredients

1 tbsp. olive oil

12 oz. chopped ham

Optional: about ¼ lb. salt pork, cut into 1-inch cubes

1 cup chopped carrots

1 cup chopped celery, plus a handful chopped celery leaves if available

1 cup chopped onion

3 cloves minced garlic

1 tsp. mustard powder (or 2 tsp. prepared Dijon mustard)

1 14-oz. can diced tomatoes, including juice, preferably fire roasted

2 bay leaves

1 tsp. dried thyme

½ tsp. ground pepper

1 lb. dry great northern or cannellini beans

1 tsp. kosher salt (eliminate if you're using salt pork)

3 cups water

3 cups chicken broth (preferably low-sodium)

12 oz. full-flavored beer

Directions

In a Dutch oven, heat olive oil. Add ham, salt pork, carrots, celery, onion, and garlic. Sauté over medium heat for several minutes, until onion is tender. Remove vegetable mixture from pan and place in crockpot. Add ingredients through pepper to crockpot mixture. Stir.

Meanwhile, rinse beans, sorting out any broken or discolored ones. In the same Dutch oven, combine beans, salt (if using), water, broth, and beer over high heat. Bring to a boil. Reduce heat to medium, cover loosely, and cook at a low boil for 10 minutes.

Add bean mixture to vegetables in crockpot, combining well. Cook on low setting for 6–8 hours, until beans are tender. Remove bay leaves and salt pork. If using salt pork, after cooling, remove fat, chop meat finely, and add to soup. Adjust seasonings.

Lighter Broccoli Cheese Soup

Makes about 8 cups

Broccoli is a top antioxidant and cancer-fighting food, with heart-healthy properties. It contains vitamins A, C, and K. Turmeric is a member of the ginger family. It has anti-inflammatory, antiviral, and antibacterial properties, and it is believed to be beneficial in fighting cancer, diabetes, and Alzheimer's disease. Citrus zests are high in fiber and flavonoids, which fight cancer and diabetes, and lower cholesterol.

Broccoli used to grow wild on Mediterranean shores. Italians were first to use it frequently; Thomas Jefferson grew it in his garden.

Note: this recipe is lighter and more "tangy" than the traditional version. To make a heartier dish, stir in half a cup of steamed rice for each serving. Top with bacon bits or chopped ham if desired. This amped-up version reminds me of a lighter broccoli-rice casserole—with no baking required!

Ingredients

2 tbsp. unsalted butter—regular or light

1 cup roughly chopped onion, preferably sweet onion

1½ lb. broccoli, cut into 1-inch or smaller pieces, stems included

6 garlic cloves, minced

2 tsp. turmeric

4 cups low-sodium chicken or vegetable broth, divided

⅓ cup dry white wine

2 tbsp. lemon juice and 2 tsp. zest, from a medium lemon

3 tbsp. plain Greek yogurt

8 oz. Velveeta or other American melting cheese, regular or low fat, cut into 6–8 pieces

Salt and pepper to taste

Directions

Melt butter in a Dutch oven over medium-low heat. Add onion; stir 1 minute. Add broccoli pieces, garlic, and turmeric. Cook, uncovered, stirring frequently, until fragrant, about 3 minutes.

Add broth, wine, and lemon juice/zest. Cover loosely and cook, stirring occasionally, until broccoli is tender, 6–8 minutes.

Stir in yogurt and Velveeta. Increase heat to medium-high, stirring until mixture boils. Turn down heat to low. Use an immersion blender to get the mixture to your desired consistency. Simmer over low heat, loosely covered, 10 minutes, allowing flavors to blend. Adjust flavors; add salt and pepper to taste. Note that soup will thicken somewhat upon standing.

Quick Corn Chowder

Makes about 6 cups/4 servings; can be doubled

Carotenoids in corn fight heart disease and cancer. This grain has more protein than many veggies. It also contains good amounts of vitamin C and fiber. Yellow corn provides eyesight benefits.

Ingredients

4–6 slices bacon, to yield about ½ cup diced bacon

2–3 red or Yukon gold potatoes (8 oz.), peeled if desired, and diced into ½-inch pieces

1 cup chopped onion

½ cup chopped celery

1 cup fresh or frozen corn kernels

3 cups chicken broth

1 14-oz. can cream-style corn

1½ tsp. garlic powder

2 tsp. Worcestershire or Pickapeppa sauce

¼ cup heavy cream or half and half

Optional: 3 tbsp. vermouth or dry sherry

Salt and pepper to taste

Optional: 1 tsp. hot sauce—more to taste

Directions

In a Dutch oven or large saucepan, preferably nonstick, sauté bacon slices over medium heat until browned and crisp, lowering temperature a bit if necessary as you turn slices. Remove and reserve slices, leaving grease in pan.

To the pan, add chopped potatoes, onions, celery, and corn kernels. Sauté 7–8 minutes, until fragrant and tender. Add broth, creamed corn, garlic powder, Worcestershire, cream, and vermouth; bring to a boil. Reduce heat to low, cover and simmer 10 minutes. Add salt, pepper, and hot sauce to taste.

Potato Leek, Cream of Asparagus, or Cream of Poblano Soup

8–10 servings

This recipe calls for pureed cauliflower, buttermilk, and broth in addition to cream. Buttermilk adds "tang" and reduces calories compared to traditional versions. All the veggies add fiber and nutrients.

For flavor variations, see notes at end of recipe.

Potato Leek Soup

3 tbsp. butter—regular or light

1 lb. leeks, cleaned and dark green sections removed

1 tsp. kosher salt, plus additional for seasoning

12–14 oz. Russet potato, cooked in microwave, about 4–6 minutes on high

10 oz. cauliflower florets, about 1 small head, roasted at 400 degrees about 20 minutes

4 cups low-sodium vegetable broth or chicken broth

1 cup heavy cream

1 cup buttermilk

Optional: ¼ cup dry white wine or sherry

Optional: 1 tsp. celery seed—more to taste

½ tsp. black or white pepper (white pepper has a more subtle flavor)

Optional: 1–2 tsp. hot sauce

Optional toppings: snipped chives or green onion, bacon bits, or a bit of pepita pesto (separate recipe)

Directions

Rinse leeks well. Chop into approximately 2-inch pieces. In a Dutch oven, over medium heat, melt butter. Add leeks and salt. Heat for 3 minutes, stirring often. Decrease heat to medium-low and cook, stirring occasionally, until leeks are tender and starting to brown, approximately 10–12 minutes.

Cool and peel the potato. To Dutch oven, add peeled potato, cauliflower, and broth, increase heat to medium-high, and bring to a boil. Add cream, buttermilk, sherry, celery seed, and pepper; reduce heat to low, cover, and gently simmer 15 minutes. Turn off heat and puree the mixture with an immersion blender until smooth. Taste and adjust seasonings if desired.

Topping

Sprinkle with chives and serve immediately, or chill and serve cold. Or try with a sprinkling of pepita pesto (separate recipe).

Cream of Asparagus Soup

Follow leek directions, substituting 1½ lb. asparagus for leeks, cutting off tough bottoms and reserving about 12 tips for garnishing. Use thin stalks if possible. Add juice and zest of 1 small lemon. Cook asparagus tips briefly in microwave: sprinkle with water and cook about 1 minute on medium setting. Add a dash of grated nutmeg for each serving, if desired.

Cream of Poblano Soup

In general, follow leek directions.

Substitutions

Sauté 1 coarsely chopped large sweet onion for leeks, adding 5 cloves sliced or chopped garlic to sauté pan. Cook in butter 5–6 minutes on medium heat, until onion begins to caramelize. Add wine; stir 30 seconds, to deglaze pan. In addition to potato, add 4 roasted poblanos, coarsely chopped, and eliminate cauliflower.

Add 1 tbsp. coriander/cilantro chutney—separate recipe—or ¼ cup cilantro leaves—and 1 tbsp. cumin instead of celery seed. After pureeing, add 1–2 tbsp. lime juice and hot sauce to taste. Serve with tortilla chips, or stir in a cup of cooked corn kernels if desired.

Red Lentil Soup with Lemon

4–6 servings

Lentils are high in protein, fiber, folate, vitamin B1, and several minerals. This healthy and colorful soup is ready in less than an hour.

Lentils were eaten thousands of years ago, and they were one of first crops domesticated in the Near East. Today, Canada is the world's largest exporter, mainly out of Saskatchewan. US production is mainly from eastern Washington state and the Idaho panhandle.

Ingredients

3 tbsp. olive oil

1 large onion, chopped

4 garlic cloves, minced

1 tbsp. tomato paste or ketchup

1 tsp. ground cumin

Kosher salt and black pepper to taste

Pinch chili powder or paprika—plus more for topping

1 quart chicken or vegetable broth

2 cups water

12 oz. light-flavored beer

1 cup red lentils, rinsed well

1 large carrot, peeled and diced

Juice of 1 medium lemon—more to taste

⅓ cup chopped cilantro, or 2–3 tsp. coriander/cilantro chutney

Directions

In a large pot, heat oil over medium heat until shimmering. Add onion and garlic; sauté until golden, about 4 minutes. Stir in tomato paste, cumin, salt, pepper, and chili powder. Sauté 2 minutes. Add broth, water, beer, lentils, and carrot. Bring to a simmer, then partially cover and turn heat to medium-low. Simmer until lentils are soft, about 30 minutes.

Stir in lemon juice and cilantro. Adjust seasonings. Sprinkle lightly with chili powder or paprika if desired.

Portuguese White Bean and Fennel Soup

Makes 10 cups, or 8 servings

Cannellini beans are a high-quality protein source. They contain many minerals, including calcium, iron, magnesium, and potassium, as well as fiber and vitamin B1. They are interchangeable with navy beans and white beans.

The pesto topping adds a colorful and tasty flavor component.

Ingredients

2 tbsp. olive oil

1½ cups chopped onion

2 tsp. kosher salt

4 garlic cloves, minced

2 tsp. fennel seeds

1 fennel bulb, diced, to yield 1½–2 cups

1 tsp. dried thyme

½ tsp. ground black pepper

1 cup diced carrots

1½ cups diced potatoes

½ cup sun-dried tomatoes, packed in oil, chopped

1 15-ounce can diced tomatoes, preferably fire-roasted, undrained

2 15-ounce cans cannellini beans, undrained
4 cups chicken or vegetable broth
Optional: ¼ cup dry vermouth

Optional: prepared green pesto or pepita pesto: store-bought or see separate recipes

Directions

Preheat oven to 350 degrees. In a Dutch oven with burner set on medium heat, warm olive oil. Add onion and salt; cook 5 minutes. Add garlic, fennel seeds, diced fennel bulb, thyme, pepper, carrots, and potatoes. Cook 5 minutes, stirring often. Remove from heat.

Stir in sun-dried tomatoes, canned tomatoes, beans, broth, and vermouth. Cover; bake for 2 hours. Stir in lemon juice. Adjust seasonings. Add a dollop of pesto to each serving.

Roasted Red Pepper-Tomato Soup
8 to 12 servings

Red bell peppers are high in antioxidants, along with vitamins A and C. They have more vitamin C than oranges. Tomatoes are rich in nutrients. They have high levels of vitamins A and C, plus potassium. Lycopene, in cooked tomatoes, has cancer-fighting properties.

 The optional pesto topping adds flavor and color.

Ingredients

1 tbsp. olive oil
3 tbsp. butter—regular or light—divided
1 medium sweet onion, peeled and chopped
4 cloves garlic, minced

3 roasted red bell peppers from a jar (water-packed), plus about 2 tbsp. liquid from jar
1 can (28 oz.) whole tomatoes such as San Marzano, undrained

1 cup tomato juice such as V-8

4-oz. piece white or whole wheat baguette or peasant bread, torn into bite-size bits

1½ tsp. smoked paprika—more to taste

3 cups low-sodium vegetable or chicken broth

2 tsp. fresh lemon juice

2 tbsp. plain Greek yogurt

1 tsp. dried basil

¼ cup dry sherry or Marsala wine

Salt and pepper to taste

Optional: 2 tsp. anchovy paste or fish sauce—for umami flavor

Optional: up to ¾ cup half and half or milk for a creamier taste

Optional: dollop of green or pepita pesto—store-bought or see separate recipes

Directions

In a Dutch oven over medium heat, combine olive oil, 1 tbsp. butter, and onion; stir often until onion is soft, about 5 minutes. Add garlic; stir for 2 minutes. Add roasted peppers and tomatoes, along with remaining ingredients through wine. Bring to a boil. Reduce heat to low and simmer 5 minutes.

Puree using a hand immersion blender. Add optional items. Cover loosely; simmer 20 minutes on low heat. Add remaining butter along with salt and pepper to taste.

Smoked Salmon Chowder

4–6 servings

Ingredients

1½ tbsp. butter

1 cup chopped onion

½ cup chopped carrot

½ cup chopped celery

1 tsp. kosher salt

2 tbsp. flour

2 tbsp. dry sherry or other dry white wine

1 12-oz. can evaporated milk

12 oz. water

1 11-oz. can corn such as Mexicorn, including liquid

1 4–5 oz. package smoked salmon

1 tsp. dried tarragon

Optional: ¼ cup chopped parsley

Directions

Melt butter in large saucepan over medium heat. Add veggies and salt; sauté until tender, about 5 minutes, stirring often. Reduce heat to medium-low. Sprinkle in flour; stir to combine. Cook for 2 minutes, stirring often. Add sherry; cook and stir 2 minutes.

Add ingredients through tarragon. Increase temperature to medium; bring to a boil, stirring often. Reduce heat to a simmer; add parsley. Cook 10 minutes to blend flavors.

Lighter Shrimp Bisque

10 servings

This recipe is lower in calories than the cream-based bisques you often find in restaurants. In addition, V-8 has many nutritional benefits since it's packed with a variety of veggies. Shrimp are high in heart-healthy omega-3s and protein, and low in fat. They contain tryptophan, which is associated with serotonin release (a mood booster), and their selenium content helps brain function.

Ingredients

2 lb. medium or large raw shrimp, bought shell-on; peeled and deveined, shells saved
1 stick (½ cup) butter, regular or light, divided
⅔ cup chopped green onion, including tops
⅔ cup chopped celery
⅓ cup all-purpose flour
3 cups shrimp stock, made with shells—see below
3 tbsp. ketchup
1 bay leaf

½ tsp. dried thyme
⅛ tsp. cayenne pepper, smoked paprika, or black pepper
1 can (12 oz.) evaporated milk
⅓ cup white wine
3 cups V-8 or Clamato juice
½ tsp. Old Bay seasoning; more to taste
Optional: sweet and spicy hot sauce such as Tiger Sauce

Directions

Follow instructions below for shrimp stock. Set aside.

Meanwhile, melt 2 tbsp. butter in a Dutch oven over medium heat. Add onion and celery; cook 5 minutes. Reduce heat to medium-low and add shrimp. Cook just until shrimp are opaque, several minutes. Do not overcook. Set aside.

Melt remaining butter in same pan over medium heat. Stir in flour; cook 3 minutes. Gradually add 3 cups prepared shrimp stock; ketchup, bay leaf, thyme, and pepper. Bring to a boil, whisking to remove any lumps. Reduce heat to low. Stir in milk, wine, and V-8 juice. Add Old Bay. Cook on low for 10 minutes. Add shrimp mixture; cook on low for 5 minutes, until shrimp are warm. Discard bay leaf. Add hot sauce.

Shrimp Stock

1 tsp. garlic powder
1 tbsp. fish sauce—found in the Asian section of most grocery stores

Shells of 2 lb. shrimp (from above)
1 tsp. Old Bay seasoning
Juice of ½ lemon

Bring all ingredients to a boil in 4 cups of water. Reduce to medium and heat 15 minutes. Discard shells.

Curried Butternut Squash Soup

About 6 servings

Butternut squash is a high-fiber, low-calorie source of vitamins A and C.

Soup can be served hot or cold. Can be made vegetarian. Pesto topping adds flavor and color.

Ingredients

1 medium butternut or similar winter squash—to yield 3 cups cooked puree

2 tbsp. vegetable or olive oil

1 cup chopped shallot or sweet onion

1 tbsp. red curry paste

1 tbsp. brown sugar

1 tbsp. grated or minced fresh ginger

Dash red pepper flakes

4 garlic cloves, chopped or sliced

3 cups chicken or vegetable broth

2 cups chopped peeled Fuji, Braeburn, or similar apple (from 2 medium apples)

⅓ cup heavy cream

1 tsp. kosher salt—to taste

Optional topping: ⅓ cup chopped fresh cilantro

Optional topping: green or pepita pesto—store bought or see separate recipes

Directions

Cut squash in half lengthwise. Scoop out and discard seeds. Place in a baking dish, flesh side down. Add about 1 inch of water. Bake at 375 degrees 45–50 minutes, until soft. Cool; scrape out flesh. Discard skin.

Meanwhile, heat oil in a Dutch oven over medium heat. Add ingredients through garlic. Cook 2 minutes, stirring frequently. Add squash, broth, and apple; bring to a boil. Add cream and salt. Cover, reduce heat; simmer 15 minutes.

Puree using a handheld immersion blender. Sprinkle each serving with toppings.

Salads

Basic Vinaigrette with Variations

Makes about ¾ cup dressing

Ingredients

¼ cup seasoned rice vinegar, cider vinegar, balsamic vinegar, or red wine vinegar

1 tsp. Dijon mustard

1 tbsp. sugar or honey—more to taste

¼ cup vegetable or olive oil (or try avocado oil or a nut-based oil such as walnut or hazelnut)

Optional: 1 small shallot, minced

Optional: 1 tsp. dried herb such as basil, thyme, marjoram, or tarragon

½ tsp. pepper

Directions

Whisk all together, or use a small food processor. Refrigerate until ready to use.

Beet Salad Vinaigrette

Add 3 tbsp. orange juice and 1 tsp. dried tarragon to basic recipe.

Apricot Vinaigrette

Add 2 tbsp. apricot jam to beet salad vinaigrette.

Lemony Vinaigrette

Follow basic instructions, using lemon or lime juice instead of vinegar. Try adding a tablespoon or two of green pesto to this recipe, for topping steamed green beans or asparagus.

Red Pepper Vinaigrette

Make basic vinaigrette using rice vinegar, eliminating the mustard and including the shallot. Add 1 roasted red bell pepper and puree using a hand immersion blender.

Pesto Vinaigrette

Follow basic recipe, using lemon juice and olive oil; add 1–2 tbsp. prepared green pesto. Try over steamed green beans, asparagus, or roasted potatoes.

Ginger Vinaigrette for Salads, Roasted or Steamed Asparagus, etc.

Follow directions for basic vinaigrette through pepper, adding 2 tbsp. minced crystallized ginger, or ginger marmalade. Optional: add 2–3 tsp. soy sauce, for Asian flavor.

Mango or Peach Slaw

Add basic dressing, made with rice vinegar, to slaw mix. Stir in 1 cup chopped mango or peach, plus ¼ cup fruit juice (such as syrup from fruit canned in its own juice), and a handful of either chopped celery or chopped bell pepper. You can also add dried fruit such as craisins, for more texture, flavor, and color.

Fruity Italian Vinaigrette

Follow directions on Good Seasons packet, substituting fruit juice for water, and adding a little honey or sugar for sweetness.

Green Apple Slaw

Serves 6-8

Ingredients

½ cup mayonnaise— regular or light
¼ cup cider vinegar
2 tsp. sugar, to taste
Optional: 1 tsp. fennel seeds, crushed, or 1
    small fennel bulb, thinly sliced
6-8 cups slaw mix
½ cup chopped green onions, both white
    and green parts
1 cup chopped celery
2 Granny Smith apples, chopped (peeled
    first if desired)
Salt and pepper to taste

Make dressing by combining ingredients through fennel. Place remaining ingredients in mixing bowl. Toss with dressing. Add salt and pepper to taste. Refrigerate at least an hour to combine flavors.

Creamy Cucumber Salad Dressing and Sauce

Makes 1 generous cup

Serving Ideas

With couscous cakes, with fried eggplant, with fried green tomatoes, over pickled beets, with salmon/crab cakes, with pan-fried tilapia, with walnut-crusted salmon, or Greek meatballs (separate recipes). Or stir into tuna salad.

Creamy Cucumber Salad

Use 1 large or 2 small cucumbers in place of grated cukes. Peel if desired; slice thinly. Process remaining ingredients; combine with sliced cukes to make a salad.

Ingredients

½ cup packed grated cucumber, which has been peeled and seeded
½ cup mayonnaise—regular or light
3 cloves garlic

3 tbsp. green onions, chopped
3 tbsp. seasoned rice vinegar—more to taste
⅓ cup buttermilk
Salt and pepper to taste

Directions

Combine ingredients in a small food processor. Add salt and pepper to taste. Chill well before serving.

Creamy Orange Avocado Salad Dressing

Makes about 1½ cups dressing

Serving Ideas

Serve over mixed greens or baby spinach, with mandarin orange or mango and thinly sliced red onion or fennel bulb, and black olives. Put a dollop over pickled beets. Try as a sauce, with cornmeal-crusted tilapia, or crab cakes. Note: you may find that this keeps in the refrigerator for up to several days without discoloring significantly, unlike some other avocado-based recipes. This may be due to the yogurt.

Avocados are a top antioxidant food, with good amounts of vitamins A and C, plus potassium, magnesium and fiber, and cholesterol-fighting power.

The Aztecs in Mexico introduced Spanish explorer Cortes to avocados in the sixteenth century.

Ingredients

3 green onions, roughly chopped
1 medium avocado, peeled and pitted
About ¾ cup orange juice, freshly squeezed—to taste

2 tbsp. plain Greek yogurt
1 tbsp. olive oil
½ tsp. kosher salt
¼ tsp. ground black pepper

Directions

Puree all ingredients in a blender or food processor until smooth.

Roasted Beet Salad with Sweet and Spicy Pecans

4–6 servings

Beets are a top antioxidant food. They are a good source of fiber, potassium, and vitamin C.

Pick and choose from the ingredients below. Use your imagination!

Ingredients

6 cups greens: baby spinach, baby kale, and arugula and/or beet greens
1 bunch fresh beets, halved if large
1 cup vinaigrette—store-bought, or see separate recipe
4 oz. crumbled Gorgonzola or goat cheese

Optional: ½ of a red onion, very thinly sliced, or ⅓ cup thinly sliced fennel bulb
Optional: ½ cup roasted pecans or sweet and spicy pecans, separate recipe
Optional: sectioned oranges, peaches, apples, or pears

Directions

Rub beets with olive oil, and wrap tightly in foil, to hasten cooking and keep them moist. Bake at 400 degrees till tender, about 45–60 minutes. Cool just until you can handle, then trim tops and bottoms, and peel. If the peel doesn't come right off, drop into ice water. Slice or cube the roasted beets. Pour vinaigrette over still-warm beets to marinate. Refrigerate at least an hour before making salad.

This doubles as **pickled beets**, for serving separately if desired. Try serving pickled beets with a dollop of sour cream and dill. Or with a dollop of goat cheese and dash of balsamic vinegar. Or try with creamy cucumber dressing, or orange-avocado dressing (separate recipes).

To make salad: If beet greens are very tender, rinse, chop and add a few to the salad for color. Layer greens, beets, and optional add-ins; top with cheese and drizzle with dressing.

 Red, white and blue salmon salad: layer onto a bed of baby spinach or baby kale: smoked salmon or roasted salmon; roasted beets; blueberries; and Feta cheese. Add a few Kalamata olives if desired. Drizzle with vinaigrette. Top with pecans.

Fresh Corn Salad

About 6 servings

Carotenoids in corn fight heart disease and cancer. This grain has more protein than many veggies. It also contains good amounts of vitamin C and fiber. Yellow corn provides an eyesight benefit.

Serving Ideas

Goes well with pan-fried fish, fish tacos, or crab cakes. Great at a summer picnic.

Ingredients

4 ears fresh corn, husked, or 4 cups canned corn, drained

1 poblano pepper or green bell pepper, diced

1 red bell pepper, diced—fresh or roasted

½ cup diced red onion

1 cup grape tomatoes, halved; or 1 cup cherry tomatoes, halved or quartered depending on size

¼ cup lime juice

2 tbsp. olive oil

Garlic salt and black pepper to taste

Optional: dash hot sauce

Directions

Fresh corn: wrap each ear of corn in a moist paper towel. Microwave on high for 3 minutes. Cool; remove kernels. Combine all ingredients; refrigerate at least an hour. Serve cool or at room temperature.

Quick Cucumber Salad

4–6 servings

Cucumbers may lower the risk of cardiovascular disease as well as several cancers, including breast, uterine, ovarian, and prostate cancers.

Serving Ideas

On sandwiches, as a condiment with BBQ, as a stand-alone salad, or on top of spinach salad. Stir into tuna salad. See below for Vietnamese sandwich.

Ingredients

⅔ cup seasoned rice vinegar

2 tbsp. vegetable or olive oil

1 tsp. kosher salt

½ tsp. black pepper

½ cup minced shallot, scallions, or red onion

Optional: 1 cup grated or julienned carrots, or minced bell pepper

2 large cucumbers, peeled if desired, thinly sliced crosswise

Optional: pinch sugar

Directions

Make a dressing by combining first 4 ingredients. Toss with vegetables. For best flavor, let stand at room temperature for 30–60 minutes, stirring several times. Refrigerate until needed.

Vietnamese-Type Banh Mi Sandwich

Include the carrots. Add about 1 tbsp. coriander or cilantro chutney—separate recipe—or up to ½ cup chopped cilantro. Spread a little more coriander chutney, red or green pesto, hummus, or a drizzle of the vinaigrette dressing on a baguette or bolillo roll. Add grilled chicken breast. If desired, drizzle with a little sesame oil or soy sauce or spread with chimichurri sauce (separate recipe). Try sandwich with a side of mango or pineapple.

Kale Salad and Kale Pesto Pasta Salad

Serves 4–6

Kale is a top antioxidant food, with high levels of vitamins A, C, K, and manganese. High in fiber, it has cholesterol-lowering benefits, making it heart-healthy. Thanks to my nutritionist friend Sue for clueing me in to the health benefits and tastiness of this kale salad several years ago!

Benjamin Franklin may have brought America's first kale seeds to the US from Scotland.

Ingredients (Basic Salad)

4 cloves garlic, minced
2 tbsp. olive oil — more to taste
2 tbsp. lemon juice or seasoned rice vinegar

Salt and fresh pepper to taste
1 bunch dark green kale, washed and dried well, thick stems removed

Directions

Cut kale leaves into small bite-sized pieces. Whisk together garlic, oil, and lemon juice. Put kale in a large bowl and toss with dressing by hand, massaging the leaves to coat them well.

Not the touchy-feely type, and don't want to "massage" the kale? In a rush? Pulse whole garlic cloves, oil and vinegar, and coarsely cut kale, in a food processor, in 2–3 batches.

Dried fruit and Nut Variation

Make basic recipe. Toss prepared kale salad with ¼ cup dried fruit—such as cherries, craisins, or apricots—¼ cup finely grated Parmesan cheese, and ¼ cup pine nuts, almonds, or walnuts, toasted if desired.

Apple-Walnut Variation

Make basic recipe. Shortly before serving, add 1 thinly sliced peeled apple (Granny Smith or Fuji), ¼ cup chopped toasted walnuts, ¼ cup thinly sliced red onion, ½ cup blue cheese crumbles, and ¼ cup chopped celery.

Fennel-Parmesan Variation

Make basic recipe. Add 1 shaved fennel bulb and ½ cup chopped fennel fronds, along with 2 oz. grated Parmesan cheese.

Honey-Pear Variation

Whisk together ½ cup pear nectar, 2 tbsp. olive oil, 2 tbsp. cider vinegar, 1–2 tbsp. honey, and 1 minced shallot. Toss with chopped kale, or pulse all ingredients in food processor. Add salt and pepper to taste.

Kale Pesto Pasta Salad

Make basic recipe in food processor; pulse to fine consistency. Meanwhile, cook 1 cup elbow or bowtie pasta according to package directions to yield about 2 cups cooked pasta. Toss kale mixture with pasta; top with 3 tbsp. roasted pine nuts or walnuts and 2 oz. grated Parmesan. Add salt and pepper to taste. Makes 4–6 servings.

Sweet Potato and Black Bean Salad

Makes 8–10 servings

Sweet potatoes contain vitamins A, B6, C, E, and several minerals. They have more beta-carotene than any other veggie, and they provide cancer-fighting benefits.

Variation: use butternut squash instead of sweet potatoes. For a fall accent, slice raw peeled sweet potato or butternut squash into about ½-inch slices. After roasting, use a mini fall-themed cookie cutter shape to make cutouts.

Sweet potatoes have been grown in Peru for thousands of years. In Shakespeare's time, they were considered an aphrodisiac.

Salad

2 lb. sweet potatoes, peeled and cut into small cubes, and tossed with 1 tbsp. olive oil
1 can black beans, drained
1 cup roasted red bell peppers, julienned into thin strips
½ cup orange juice, preferably fresh
½ cup chopped red onion
2 scallions, both white and green parts, chopped

Dressing

½ tsp. paprika, preferably smoked Spanish paprika
¼ cup olive oil
3 cloves minced garlic
⅓ cup red wine vinegar
Dash hot pepper sauce
Optional: 2 tbsp. chopped cilantro or 2 tsp. coriander/cilantro chutney
Salt and black pepper to taste

Directions

Place oiled sweet potato bits on a parchment-lined cookie sheet. Sprinkle with salt. Roast at 400 degrees till soft and starting to brown, about 20 minutes.

In a mixing bowl, combine remaining ingredients through scallions. When potatoes are cool, add them to black bean mixture.

Combine dressing ingredients in a jar; shake well. Dress the salad. Add cilantro and salt and pepper to taste. Refrigerate at least an hour to combine flavors. Serve slightly cool or at room temperature.

Breads

Sweet Potato Knot Rolls

Makes 2–3 dozen rolls; can be frozen after baking

Sweet potatoes contain vitamins A, B6, C, E, and several minerals; they have more beta-carotene than any other veggie, and they provide cancer-fighting benefits.

Ingredients

1 package active dry yeast

1½ cups warm milk

1 tsp. honey or sugar

1½ cups cooked and mashed sweet potatoes

6 tbsp. butter—regular or light—melted, cooled slightly, and divided

4 cups all-purpose flour mixed with 3 tbsp. vital wheat gluten; or use 4 cups bread flour

1½ tsp. kosher salt

2 large egg yolks, lightly beaten

Directions

In a small bowl or liquid measuring cup, dissolve yeast in mixture of milk and honey. Let stand 10 minutes. Pour into bowl of a stand mixer. Add sweet potatoes, 4 tbsp. butter, salt, and egg yolks, using a wooden spoon to combine.

Whisk together flour, gluten, and salt. If using bread flour, combine bread flour and salt. Gradually add flour mixture to potato mixture until a soft dough forms, using a wooden spoon or your hands. Divide dough into two equal pieces.

Using a dough hook, knead half of dough until smooth and elastic, about 5 minutes. Or you can knead by hand about 8 minutes. Repeat with other half. Add more flour, 1 tablespoon at a time, if needed, to prevent dough from sticking to dough hook or fingers.

Transfer dough to two bowls coated with cooking spray, turning to coat top. Let rise in a warm place 45 minutes or until doubled in size. Punch dough down. Let rest 5 minutes.

Line two baking sheets with parchment paper. Divide each half of dough into 12–18 equal portions. Shape each portion into 7–9-inch ropes. Shape each rope into a knot; tuck top end of knot under roll. Place rolls on prepared pans. Lightly coat rolls with cooking spray; cover and let rise in a warm place for 30 minutes or until doubled in size.

Preheat oven to 375 degrees. Bake rolls for 10 minutes. Rotate pans; bake an additional 8–10 minutes or until rolls are golden brown on top and sound hollow when tapped. Remove rolls from pans; place on wire racks. Brush rolls with remaining butter. Serve warm or at room temperature.

Corn and Poblano Spoon Bread

About 12 casserole servings or 18 muffins

Carotenoids in corn fight heart disease and cancer. This grain has more protein than many veggies. It also contains good amounts of vitamin C and fiber. Yellow corn provides an eyesight benefit. Corn meal is a good source of fiber and some antioxidants.

Bite-Sized Corndog Mini-Muffins

Use a mini muffin pan. Place small slices of smoked sausage on top of muffins before baking. Baking time: 15–17 minutes.

Ingredients

1 cup cornmeal

1 tsp. baking powder

1 tsp. baking soda

1 tsp. kosher salt

2 large eggs, beaten lightly

¼ cup milk or cream

1 14-oz. can creamed corn

1 11-oz. can Mexicorn, drained

4 cloves garlic, minced

3 tbsp. olive or vegetable oil

1–2 roasted poblano peppers, peeled, seeded, and chopped finely, to yield about ½ cup (use somewhat less for a milder flavor or use canned green chiles)

4 oz. grated Pepper Jack, Colby, or Cheddar cheese (or use a mixture)

Directions

Preheat oven to 375 degrees. Coat a 9x13 inch casserole dish or other large baking dish with nonstick spray. Or use a muffin tin, preferably with paper liners.

Whisk together dry ingredients. Stir in remaining ingredients, reserving about ¼ cup grated cheese. Pour into casserole dish. Sprinkle with remaining cheese.

Bake 40–50 minutes, until center is firm and casserole is beginning to turn golden. Muffins will take about 25–30 minutes.

Blueberry-Lemon Scones

Makes 12–24

Traditionally, British scones are made using moderate amounts of milk and (sometimes) egg. They are served with preserves and clotted cream, which can be hard to find in the United States. I have found that adding heavy cream to the dough works well in the food processor method below, and the fruity glaze fills out the flavor.

For a flavor variation, substitute chopped dried apricots or cherries for the blueberries.

Dough

¾ cup dried blueberries or blueberry-flavored
    dried cranberries
1 tsp. vanilla
½ cup chilled heavy cream
2¼ cups all-purpose flour

2 tsp. baking powder
1 tsp. salt
½ cup sugar
6 tbsp. butter, chilled and cut into small pieces

3 tbsp. shortening, chilled and cut into small pieces

¼ cup lemon juice
1 tbsp. lemon zest

Glaze

1 cup powdered sugar
2 tbsp. fresh lemon juice

1 tsp. vanilla

Directions

For dough, combine dried blueberries, vanilla, and cream. Set aside. Combine dry ingredients through sugar in food processor. Pulse several times. Add shortening and butter; pulse until it becomes a coarse meal.

Pour berry/cream mixture into flour mixture, then drizzle with lemon juice, and add zest. Pulse about 8–10 times, until mixture forms one or two clumps.

Dump onto a floured surface. Roll out to about ½ inch depth. Make shapes using a cookie cutter.

Bake at 400 degrees for 12–14 minutes, making sure not to burn bottoms. Meanwhile, whisk together glaze ingredients. Drizzle over warm scones.

Overnight Buttermilk Sweet or Savory Rolls

Makes 2–3 dozen rolls

I like this recipe because you can make the dough anywhere from two to twenty-four hours before baking, and no kneading is required! Let the mixer do the work.

For savory rolls, such as pesto or cheese-filled rolls, and for pretzel rolls, see notes at end of sweet roll recipe.

Ingredients

1 package very active dry yeast

2 tbsp. granulated sugar (1 tbsp. for savory rolls)

8 tbsp. (1 stick) butter for dough, plus 5 tbsp. butter for topping (2 tbsp. for savory topping)

1 cup buttermilk

2½ cups all-purpose flour, plus more as needed for patting out dough

1 tsp. kosher salt

1 tsp. baking soda

⅓ cup packed brown sugar

1 tsp. ground cinnamon—or for a change, try ginger, especially if using orange-vanilla glaze

½ tsp. ground nutmeg

Optional: 1 small peeled and diced apple or pear, ½ cup chopped nuts

Optional: orange-vanilla or caramel glaze (separate recipes)

Directions

Place yeast and sugar in bottom of stand mixer bowl. Cut 1 stick butter into 6–8 pieces. Heat buttermilk and cut-up butter in a small heavy saucepan over very low heat, just until butter has melted. Pour over yeast mixture; whisk to mix. Let stand 10 minutes. Meanwhile, put 3 tbsp. additional butter in freezer.

In another large bowl, whisk together flour, salt, and baking soda. Using a wooden spoon or large spatula, stir flour mixture into buttermilk mixture, until a soft dough forms.

Using an electric mixer, beat on medium speed 3 minutes. Set aside for 20 minutes at room temperature.

Meanwhile, in a small bowl, mix brown sugar with spices. Chop apples. On lightly floured parchment paper, pat out dough into a rectangle about 10x13. Cut into quadrants. Sprinkle brown sugar mixture over dough, leaving a border of at least ½ inch. Grate frozen 3 tbsp. butter onto top. Add apples and nuts.

For savory rolls, eliminate brown sugar and spices. Roll out dough into rectangle, then quadrants; use chosen filling. Roll up each quadrant into a log, using the long sides and tucking in filling. Use bench knife if it helps. Coat with nonstick spray to prevent drying out. Cover and refrigerate logs for at least 2 hours and up to 24 hours.

The next morning, bake the rolls. Preheat oven to 375 degrees. While oven is heating, slice logs into about ¾-inch pieces and place, cut sides up, on a parchment- or foil-lined cookie sheet, leaving a little room between each one. Melt remaining 2 tbsp. butter and brush onto tops. Bake in preheated oven 20–25 minutes, until starting to brown on top. While still warm, drizzle with glaze if using.

For savory pesto-, tapenade-, or cheese-filled rolls, follow directions above, reducing sugar to 1 tbsp. and butter to 1 stick plus 2 tbsp. For filling, use 1 cup prepared pesto or tapenade (drained well to reduce liquid) or 2 cups grated cheese. After cutting logs, bake either cut-side up or standing upright. Brush with 2 tbsp. melted butter before baking. See separate recipes for pesto and tapenade.

For pretzel rolls, reduce yeast to 1 tsp. Eliminate baking soda. Follow savory instructions through 20-minute dough rest. Refrigerate dough in a single ball.

The next day, pinch off 10–12 balls. Preheat oven to 450 degrees. Bring 8 cups water and ½ cup baking soda to rolling boil in large saucepan. Dust each dough piece with flour; roll into a ball in hands.

Roll out each dough piece into about an 8-inch strand; fold into pretzel shapes. Drop several at a time into boiling water; remove when they rise to top of water, about 30 seconds. Place on parchment-lined baking sheet. Dust with kosher salt. Bake about 12 minutes, checking after 10 minutes and rotating pan if necessary.

For a twist on the breakfast sandwich, cut roll in half and stack with fillings of your choice, such as scrambled egg, bacon, and cheese.

Peach, Pear, or Mango Bread

Makes 1 large loaf or 3–4 small loaves

For mango bread with a special twist that is good for the holidays, make mango-craisin bread. To the dough, add a mixture of ¾ cup dried cranberries (soaked in ¼ cup brandy, cognac, or triple sec for at least 15 minutes.) Frost with orange-vanilla glaze, including ginger.

Ingredients

2 cups chopped fresh or frozen peaches, mangoes, or pears (about 2 medium)

¼ cup orange juice (for pear, substitute ¼ cup buttermilk)

½ cup butter, softened

1 cup sugar

1 tsp. vanilla extract

3 large eggs

2½ cups all-purpose flour

1 tsp. baking powder

½ tsp. baking soda

1 tsp. salt

1 tsp. ground cinnamon (or ½ tsp. nutmeg and ½ tsp. cardamom)

Optional: 1 cup chopped nuts

Optional for peach or mango bread: orange-vanilla glaze (separate recipe)

Directions

Toss fruit with juice or buttermilk. Set aside. Cream butter; gradually add sugar and vanilla, mixing well. Add eggs, one at a time, beating well after each addition.

Mix together all remaining dry ingredients; add to creamed mixture alternately with fruit mixture. Add optional nuts. Pour batter into a greased and floured large loaf pan, filling no more than ⅔ full. If you have extra batter, make a mini-loaf or some muffins.

Bake at 350 degrees for 1 hour or until wooden pick inserted in center comes out clean. Small loaves take about 40 minutes (muffins take about 20 minutes). Cool in pan for 10 minutes. Remove from loaf pan and cool completely. Drizzle with glaze if desired.

Pumpkin Apple Bread

Makes 2 large loaves or 6 small loaves

Serving option

Orange curd (separate recipe) is a tasty accompaniment.

Topping

1 tbsp. all-purpose flour

¼ cup granulated sugar

1 tsp. ground cinnamon

1 tbsp. cold unsalted butter

Dry Ingredients

3 cups all-purpose flour

1 tsp. kosher salt

2 tsp. baking soda

1 tsp. ground cinnamon

1 tsp. freshly grated nutmeg

½ tsp. ground cloves

½ tsp. ground allspice

Wet Ingredients

1 15–oz. can solid-pack pumpkin puree (not pumpkin pie mix)

½ cup vegetable oil

2 cups granulated sugar

4 large eggs, lightly beaten

2 apples (Braeburn, Fuji, or Granny Smith) peeled, cored, and grated: about 2 generous cups

Directions

To make topping, use a pastry blender to combine flour, sugar, cinnamon, and butter in a small bowl, or use two knives, until mixture resembles coarse meal. Set aside.

To make bread, put a rack in middle of oven and preheat oven to 350 degrees. Grease two 9x5 inch loaf pans or 6 small pans. Set aside. Whisk together flour, salt, baking soda, cinnamon, nutmeg, cloves, and allspice in a medium bowl. Whisk together pumpkin, oil, sugar, and eggs in a large bowl.

Gradually add flour mixture to wet mixture, stirring until well combined. Fold in apples. Divide batter between buttered loaf pans. Sprinkle topping evenly over each loaf. Bake until a wooden pick or skewer inserted in center of bread comes out clean, 50–60 minutes for large loaves, and 35–40 minutes for small loaves. Cool loaves in pans on a rack for 45 minutes, then turn out onto rack and cool completely, about 1 hour.

Breakfast, Brunch, and Lunch

Granola Bars

Makes 30–40 bars

These make a quick breakfast, served as bars or crumbled onto yogurt with fresh fruit mixed in. See recipe below for granola parfait. Or serve later in the day, over ice cream.

Oats are a good source of fiber, help manage blood sugar, and strengthen bones. The fruit, nut butter, and nuts are an added bonus, for protein and fiber. Pepitas (pumpkin seeds) are a good source of fiber, protein, and several minerals. Beneficial in the creation of serotonin, they can elevate one's mood.

Ingredients

3 cups quick-cooking oats (the 1-minute kind, not instant)

⅔ cup creamy peanut butter or almond butter (softened in microwave if very stiff)

2 cups lightly toasted nuts: slivered almonds, pecans, walnuts, and/or pistachios, coarsely chopped

1 cup roasted/salted pepitas

1 cup shredded coconut

½ cup lightly packed brown sugar

1 tsp. salt

⅓ cup maple syrup

½ cup melted butter

1 cup dried fruit such as cranberries, cherries, or mangoes (coarsely chopped if large like cherries)

⅓ cup honey

Directions

Preheat oven to 350 degrees. Toast oats on a cookie sheet for 10–12 minutes, or until just golden on the edges. While warm, toss with almond butter in a large bowl. Add all other ingredients. Press ingredients firmly onto a parchment-lined cookie sheet, using a heavy pan such as another cookie sheet.

Cook for 18–20 minutes, until very fragrant and browning on the edges. Cool completely, then cut into bars or break into crumbles.

Personal Granola Parfaits

Using individual cups or glasses, layer 2 tbsp. yogurt, 2 tbsp. granola, and 2 tbsp. fruit. Repeat until glass is filled. Drizzle with honey if desired.

Raspberry and Mascarpone Breakfast Strata

Serves 12

A breakfast/brunch version of bread pudding—use your favorite preserves.

For flexibility, you may refrigerate overnight before baking.

Ingredients

1 lb. day-old challah or Hawaiian bread, torn into bite-size pieces

6 large eggs, divided

1 cup evaporated milk or half and half

¼ cup buttermilk (for tang)

1 cup heavy cream

¼ cup granulated sugar, divided

2 tsp. vanilla extract

½ tsp. ground nutmeg

½ tsp. kosher salt

8 oz. mascarpone cheese

8 oz. cream cheese, softened

4 tbsp. unsalted butter, softened

¼ cup raspberry- or orange-flavored liqueur (or orange juice)

2 cups raspberry jam or preserves, heated in microwave or stovetop to a syrupy consistency

Powdered sugar, for dusting

Directions

Preheat oven to 325 degrees. Spread bread cubes on two cookies sheets and bake about 8 minutes, until fragrant and just starting to brown. Remove from oven. Coat a 9x13 baking dish with cooking spray. Arrange half the bread in dish, overlapping and wedging pieces to cover the bottom.

For custard, whisk together 5 of the 6 eggs in a large bowl. Add evaporated milk, buttermilk, cream, 2 tbsp. sugar, vanilla, nutmeg, and salt. Pour half the custard over bread in baking dish, letting it soak in thoroughly. Mash down to create a flat surface. Set remaining custard aside.

For the filling, use a handheld or stand mixer to beat together mascarpone, cream cheese, butter, remaining egg, and remaining 2 tbsp. sugar in a large bowl until soft and fluffy, about 1 minute. Beat in liqueur or orange juice.

Drop half the filling over soaked bread, gently spreading it out. Drizzle half the jam on top. Arrange remaining bread in a layer, then repeat process with custard, cheese filling, and jam.

Bake strata immediately, or cover and refrigerate overnight.

Bake 40–50 minutes, or until the strata is puffed, firmly set, and starting to brown. Refrigerated strata may take up to 60 minutes. Let cool 10 minutes; sprinkle with powdered sugar.

Black Bean and Pepper Jack Burgers

6 servings

Black beans provide potassium, fiber, calcium, magnesium, B1, B6, and iron.

For garbanzo bean burgers, substitute garbanzo beans for black beans, parsley for cilantro, and marjoram or thyme for cumin. These are similar to Greek falafel patties.

Ingredients

1 cup mashed russet potato, cooked in microwave then peeled and mashed; or 1½ cups hydrated bulgur wheat, prepared with ¾ cup dry bulgur as directed below
4 whole cloves garlic, peeled

2 large scallions (or 1–2 slices red onion)
1 bell pepper or poblano pepper, coarsely chopped
1 15–oz. can black beans, drained thoroughly
1 large egg

¼ cup chopped fresh cilantro or parsley, or 1 tbsp. cilantro/coriander chutney

2 tbsp. olive oil, divided

1 tsp. ground cumin, oregano, or marjoram

1 tsp. kosher salt and black pepper to taste

2 oz. finely grated pepper jack or other white cheese

Optional sauces: Salsa, creamy cucumber sauce, pesto, chili lime sauce, red chile-pepita sauce, or chimichurri (separate recipes)

Optional garnishes: Sliced avocado, tomato, or a dollop of guacamole

Directions

Prepare potato or bulgur filler. For potato, in a medium bowl, mash potato to yield ¾ cup. For bulgur, rinse ¾ cup raw bulgur thoroughly. Place in small bowl and pour in 1 cup boiling water. Let stand 30 minutes. Drain.

To prepare veggie mixture, put garlic, onion, and bell pepper in food processor. Pulse several times to chop coarsely. To food processor, add beans, egg, cilantro, 1 tbsp. oil, cumin, salt/pepper, and grated cheese. Pulse several more times to combine, while leaving mixture chunky.

Stir potato or bulgur mixture into veggie mixture. Form into 5 or 6 half-inch thick patties and transfer to a parchment-lined plate. Refrigerate for at least 30 minutes to firm up the burgers.

In a rush? You can eliminate the refrigeration, spray tops with olive oil, and bake at 350 degrees for 25 minutes; then flip, spray tops with oil, and bake another 5–6 minutes, until firm. Note that the baking method is best suited to bulgur version.

For stovetop cooking, heat a large heavy-duty skillet or griddle on medium heat until very hot. Add 1 tbsp. oil and swirl the pan to coat the bottom, or spray on oil with a mister. Cook the burgers until browned, with a good crust, and cooked through, 5–6 minutes per side, checking after 4 minutes to make sure burgers aren't burning.

Greek Pasta Salad

10–12 servings

The amounts below are just guidelines; adjust to your taste. I like this recipe because it is flexible, filling, and packed with tasty and nutritious veggies.

Dressing

1 cup prepared lemony vinaigrette (see separate recipe). Add 1 tsp. dried marjoram or oregano if you like.

Salad

16 oz. oz. spiral, rotini, shell, or elbow-shaped pasta, cooked according to package directions

4 green onions, chopped (white and light green parts)

4 Roma tomatoes, seeded and chopped (or 2 cups halved grape or cherry tomatoes)

2–3 stalks celery, chopped

1 large or 2 medium cucumbers (peeled, seeded, and chopped)

½ cup finely chopped fresh parsley, preferably flat-leaf

8 oz. Feta cheese, crumbled

About 2 dozen Kalamata olives in water brine, pitted (and up to 3 tbsp. of brine reserved)

Optional: 10–12 pickled pepperoncini peppers, minced

Salt, pepper, and smoked paprika to taste.

Directions

Pour dressing over warm pasta; stir well. Let cool at least 5 minutes, stirring several times. Meanwhile, combine remaining ingredients. Combine with dressed pasta. Adjust seasonings. Add olive brine if desired. Cover, and refrigerate at least 2 hours, until flavors are blended.

Mains

Butternut Squash and Kale Lasagna

About 12 servings

Butternut squash is a high-fiber, low-calorie source of vitamins A and C. Kale is a top antioxidant food, with high levels of vitamins A, C, K, and manganese. High in fiber, it has cholesterol-fighting benefits and is heart-healthy.

Ingredients

1 butternut squash or similar winter squash, to yield 2 cups puree

½ cup ricotta cheese

1 large egg, beaten

2 tsp. dried sage

1 tsp. kosher salt and ½ tsp. white or black pepper

2 cups prepared béchamel or use kohlrabi puree (separate recipes)

1 bunch kale, tough stems removed, leaves rinsed, and chopped coarsely

12 oz. pear nectar or apple cider

1 shallot, minced

12 oz. sweet Italian sausage, removed from casings (for a vegetarian version, use 12 oz. sliced button mushrooms)

8 oz. grated white cheese such as Fontina or mozzarella cheese

6 no-boil lasagna noodles (about half a 9-oz. box)

Directions

Cut squash in half lengthwise. Scoop out seeds. Place in baking pan, flesh sides down. Add about 1 inch water. Bake at 375 degrees 45–50 minutes, or until soft. Cool; scrape out flesh to yield 2 cups. Stir in ricotta, egg, sage, salt, and pepper.

Meanwhile, use a food processor to combine stemmed kale, nectar, and shallot. Or chop finely by hand the kale and shallot. Cook kale, nectar, and shallot in a saucepan over medium heat, uncovered, until tender, 10–15 minutes. Move to a large bowl, along with any liquid.

Using same pan, heat sausage or mushrooms over medium heat. Cook 6–8 minutes, until cooked through. Turn off heat and discard visible grease from sausage. Add sausage or mushrooms to kale mixture.

In a greased casserole dish, assemble layers as listed below. Let sit 10 minutes. Cover; cook at 375 for 30 minutes. Uncover and bake 10–15 minutes longer, until bubbly and beginning to brown.

Layers

First layer: béchamel (⅓), noodles (½), kale/sausage mixture (½), squash (½), cheese (½)
Second layer: béchamel (⅓), noodles (remaining ½), kale/sausage mixture (remaining ½), squash (remaining ½)
Third layer: béchamel (remaining ⅓)
Topping: cheese (remaining ½), for sprinkling on top

Classic Crab Cakes

6–8 servings

This recipe can also be used for leftover cooked fish such as cod, salmon, or tilapia.

Serving Ideas

Serve with hollandaise, remoulade, red bell pepper pesto, creamy cucumber dressing, chili-lime sauce, orange-avocado sauce, or mango salsa.

Crab is a good source of calcium, magnesium, and protein. Citrus zests are high in fiber and flavonoids, which fight cancer and diabetes, and they lower cholesterol.

The idea of making meat pies goes back to ancient times. Recipes similar to modern crab cakes go back to colonial times.

Ingredients

2 tbsp. sour cream or plain Greek yogurt (more if needed)

¼ cup diced celery (for a spicier effect, try 3 tbsp. minced poblano or jalapeno pepper)

⅓ cup minced green onions, both white and green parts

2 large eggs, lightly beaten

1 cup crushed crackers such as saltines (about 24 crackers) or use dry breadcrumbs such as panko

2 tbsp. fresh lemon juice or lime juice

2 tsp. lemon zest or lime zest

2 tsp. prepared horseradish

2 tsp. seafood seasoning such as Old Bay

½ tsp. black pepper

1 tsp. hot sauce such as Tiger Sauce—more to taste—or your favorite (preferably sweet/spicy)

1 lb. fresh lump crabmeat or cooked cod or salmon

2 tbsp. butter

2 tbsp. olive oil or vegetable oil

Preparation

Combine ingredients through hot sauce in a medium bowl. Fold in crabmeat. Shape mixture into 8–12 balls using palms of hands, then press into patties. Chill at least 30 minutes. If mixture doesn't hold together, add a little more sour cream or yogurt.

Heat half the butter with half the oil in a large skillet over medium heat. Add half the crab cakes, and cook about 3 minutes on first side, until golden, checking after about 2½ minutes. Turn over; cook 2–3 minutes. Repeat with remaining crab cakes.

Braised Cod with Pesto

4 servings

Ingredients

2 tbsp. olive oil

2 medium onions, thinly sliced

1 tsp. oregano or marjoram

Salt and pepper to taste

½ cup dry white wine

1 cup chicken or seafood broth

2 medium tomatoes, chopped

4 6-ounce pieces skinless cod, halibut or haddock

½ cup prepared pesto

Directions

Heat oil in a large skillet over medium heat. Add onion and marjoram. Cook 5 minutes, stirring often. Add wine and broth; cook another 5 minutes, until somewhat reduced in volume.

Add tomatoes. Season the fish with salt. Cover and simmer until fish is opaque throughout, 8 to 12 minutes. Adjust seasonings.

Combine pesto with ¼ cup cooking juice; more if desired. Serve fish with tomatoes and broth, discarding onions if desired. Drizzle pesto mixture over individual servings.

Cornmeal-Crusted Tilapia with Choice of Sauces

6 servings

Tilapia is a low-calorie, very good source of protein and magnesium, vitamin B12, and vitamin D. If you are concerned about safety due to conditions under which your store's tilapia was raised, use a similar fish such as swai or flounder.

Serving Ideas

Try a sauce such as orange-avocado; hollandaise; béarnaise, remoulade, red bell pepper pesto; chimichurri; creamy cucumber; or chili-lime sauce. Leftovers? Make fish tacos. Toss shredded lettuce with chili-lime sauce; top with cooked tilapia pieces. Add chopped tomato if desired.

Ingredients

½ cup cornmeal or finely crushed tortilla chips

½ tsp. Creole seasoning such as Tony Chachere's, or salt and pepper to taste

6 4-oz. tilapia or flounder fillets

1 egg, beaten

1 tbsp. unsalted butter—regular or light—plus more as needed

1 tablespoon olive oil—more as needed

Directions

Stir seasonings into cornmeal. Place in a shallow dish. Place beaten egg in another shallow dish. Wash filets and pat dry. Dip fish into beaten egg, covering both sides of fillets. Dredge egg-coated fish in seasoned cornmeal, shaking off excess. Discard excess cornmeal.

Heat olive oil and butter in a skillet 1–2 minutes over medium heat, until sizzling. Cook fish until golden, turning once, 6–8 minutes total. Check at 3 minutes. Add more oil and butter between batches, if needed. Serve with the sauce of your choice, or simply sprinkle with lemon or lime juice.

Walnut-crusted Salmon with Creamy Cucumber Sauce

4 servings

Salmon is a very good source of protein, potassium, magnesium, vitamins B6 and B12, and Omega-3s, which help brain function and skin health. Walnuts are also a good source of Omega-3s and fiber.

Variation

Instead of walnuts, use Spanish almond topping (separate recipe).

Ingredients

1 lb. salmon filets

2–3 tbsp. mayonnaise (enough to coat filets)—
    regular or light—or use aioli (separate recipe)

½ cup finely chopped walnuts

¼ cup panko breadcrumbs

1 tbsp. melted butter

½ tsp. each salt and pepper—more to taste

Creamy cucumber sauce (separate recipe)

Directions

Preheat oven to 400 degrees. Spread filets with mayonnaise. Combine walnuts, panko, butter, salt, and pepper in a small bowl. Press into filets. Bake for 12–14 minutes, depending on thickness of filets, until fish flakes easily with a fork.

Sweet and Spicy Seared Salmon

4 servings

Salmon is a very good source of protein, potassium, magnesium, vitamins B6 and B12, and Omega 3s, which help brain function and skin health.

Serving Ideas

Serve over a roasted beet salad, below, with blueberry sauce, or with apricot pepper preserves (separate recipes).

Ingredients

16 oz. salmon filets, preferably skin on, cut into 4 pieces

2 tsp. Cajun spice such as Tony Chachere's

2 tbsp. brown sugar

¼ cup peach or apricot preserves (½ cup if making beet salad)

1 tbsp. lime juice (2 tbsp. if making beet salad)

2 tbsp. olive oil

Directions

Preheat oven to 300 degrees, for the step after searing. Whisk together preserves and lime juice; set aside.

Combine Cajun spice and brown sugar; press into flesh side of salmon. If salmon is skinless, coat both sides. Heat a heavy pan, preferably nonstick, over medium high heat for 2 minutes. Add oil and heat 1 minute. Add salmon, skin side down. Cook 2 minutes skin-side down. Carefully turn over, turn down heat to medium, and sear flesh side for another 2 minutes, checking after 90 seconds to make sure topping isn't burning. If fish is skinless, cook 2 minutes on first side and 1 minute on second side.

Slide filets onto a baking pan; drizzle with glaze. Bake until done, 5–7 minutes at 300 degrees. Fish should flake after resting. If salmon needs more cooking, use microwave. Cook at medium-high speed using 30 second intervals.

Beet Salad for Seared Salmon
4 servings

Ingredients

2 beets, roasted (wrap in foil; bake at 400 degrees 45–60 minutes, until tender; cool and peel)

Optional: 2 sliced peaches or oranges

3 cups mixed field greens, arugula, or kale

Optional: 1 cup crumbled Cotija or Feta cheese

Optional: halved Kalamata olives

Optional: ⅓ cup roasted, salted pepitas or pistachios

3 tbsp. balsamic vinegar, for drizzling

Greek Shrimp with Feta and Tomato

4–6 servings

Serve over rice or with roasted potatoes

Ingredients

1 tbsp. olive oil

1 medium onion, finely chopped

5 garlic cloves, minced

2 tsp. dried marjoram or oregano

2 14-oz. cans diced tomatoes, preferably fire-roasted, undrained

⅓ cup dry white wine

⅓ cup pitted Kalamata olives from a jar, plus 3 tbsp. brine

1 lb. uncooked medium or large shrimp, peeled and deveined

¾ cup crumbled Feta or Cotija cheese

Optional: red pepper flakes, to taste

Optional: several dashes of lemon juice or red wine vinegar

Salt and pepper to taste

Directions

In a large nonstick skillet, heat oil over medium heat. Add onion; cook and stir 5 minutes or until tender. Add garlic and marjoram; cook 1 minute longer. Stir in tomatoes and wine. Bring to a boil. Reduce heat; simmer, uncovered, 5–7 minutes or until sauce is slightly thickened.

Add shrimp; cook 5–6 minutes or until shrimp turn pink, stirring occasionally. Remove from heat; sprinkle with cheese.

Crockpot French Dip Sandwich and French Onion Soup

Serves 8–10

Two meals in one! My friend Amy, who has a refined palate and is an expert cook, swears by the balsamic vinegar on this and other dishes, to add a layer of flavor. She recommends including the vermouth. She suggests serving with slaw, on the side or layered into the sandwich. This soup freezes well.

Ingredients

2½–3 lb. trimmed beef brisket, cut into two pieces if necessary for browning

⅓ cup flour, seasoned with 2 tsp. salt and 1 tsp. pepper

2 tbsp. olive or vegetable oil

¼ cup wine or vermouth, for deglazing pan

3 cups low-sodium beef broth (increase to 8 cups if you want to make French onion soup, below)

1 sweet onion, sliced (use 3 onions to make soup)

4 cloves garlic, minced (use 6 cloves to make soup)

3 tbsp. Worcestershire sauce (use ¼ cup plus 1 tbsp. to make soup)

Optional: drizzle of balsamic vinegar—to taste

Salt and pepper to taste

Optional, for French onion soup: baguette slices and Swiss or Gruyere, per directions below

Directions

Rub brisket with seasoned flour. In a heavy pan, such as a Dutch oven, brown beef in 1 tbsp. oil over medium-high heat for about 4 minutes per side, adding oil as necessary. Place half the onions in a slow cooker. Cover with beef; add remaining onions. Scrape up any browned bits from pan and add them, too, using wine or vermouth to deglaze.

Using emptied Dutch oven, combine broth, garlic, and Worcestershire sauce. Pour gravy over beef and onion mixture in crockpot. Cover and cook until very tender, on high for about 5 hours, or low for 8 hours. Let rest at least 10 minutes. Transfer brisket to a cutting board and thinly slice against the grain.

Optional: drizzle with balsamic vinegar before serving with gravy. This adds another layer of flavor.

French Onion Soup

For 4 servings, and a traditional presentation, follow directions above, using larger amounts of indicated soup ingredients. You will need 4 to 6-oz. Swiss or similar cheese, sliced, and 4–8 baguette slices to fit over oven-safe soup bowls or crocks. Fill bowls about ⅔ with soup. Toast baguette slices lightly. Place toasted bread slices on top of soup, add cheese, and broil until bubbly.

For a shortcut, try dipping Parmesan garlic bread—homemade or store-bought—into broth.

Hanukkah Brisket

8–10 servings

I like the flexibility of using a Dutch oven or crockpot and the tasty, thick gravy, made by pureeing the veggie toppings.

Ingredients

4 lb. trimmed brisket

3 tbsp. flour seasoned with 1 tsp. kosher salt and 1 tsp. pepper

3 tbsp. olive or vegetable oil, divided

1 oz. dried porcini mushrooms, hydrated in 2 cups boiling water for 20 minutes (liquid reserved)

4 onions—preferably sweet onions—thickly sliced

5 cloves minced garlic

1 10-oz. can condensed French onion soup, undiluted

1 cup dry red wine

1 cup mushroom broth, from hydrating mushrooms

½ cup marinated sun-dried tomatoes, drained and coarsely chopped

2 tbsp. balsamic vinegar

2 tsp. dried thyme

Directions

Preheat oven to 325 degrees, or use crockpot. Rub brisket with seasoned flour. In a Dutch oven, heat 2 tbsp. oil over medium heat. Sear brisket all over, about 5 minutes per side. Move to a platter or crockpot.

Reduce heat to medium-low. Add 1 tbsp. oil and onions. Sauté until golden, 12–15 minutes. Add garlic; cook 2 minutes. Place brisket on top of onions in Dutch oven, and add remaining ingredients, including mushroom broth; or place onions, then beef and remaining ingredients in crockpot.

On a stovetop, bring mixture to a boil over medium-high heat, then cover and cook in oven 3½–4 hours.

In a crockpot, cook on high for 4–5 hours, or on low for 8–9 hours.

Cook brisket until falling-apart tender. Allow to cool at least 30 minutes before cutting. Slice against the grain. Meanwhile, skim fat from sauce. Puree strained sauce using an immersion blender.

Coffee and Balsamic Marinated Steak

4 servings

This recipe is simple and satisfying. You can use an indoor grill if desired.

Serving Idea

Serve with spicy pecan bacon (see sweet and spicy pecan recipe for details).

Ingredients

1 lb. boneless steaks, such as petite sirloin or rib eye

5 cloves garlic, minced

1 teaspoon dried thyme

1 tsp. onion salt

1 cup strong brewed coffee, cooled to room temperature

¼ cup balsamic vinegar, divided

1 tsp. kosher salt

1 tsp. freshly ground black pepper

1 tsp. granulated sugar

2 tbsp. butter, softened

Directions

Poke holes in steak. Place in a gallon Ziploc bag. Combine garlic, thyme, onion salt, coffee, and 2 tbsp. vinegar. Pour over steaks; marinate in refrigerator at least 30 minutes and up to 8 hours, turning once or twice.

Heat a grill or cast iron skillet for 5 minutes on medium-high heat. Combine black pepper, sugar, and kosher salt. Remove steaks from marinade; discard marinade. Dry with paper towels, then rub with pepper mixture.

Coat grill with nonstick spray. Grill 4–5 minutes per side, depending on thickness of steaks and desired degree of cooking. While still hot, top with softened butter and drizzle with remaining 2 tbsp. vinegar. Cool at least 10 minutes before cutting or serving.

Greek Meatballs or Sliders

Serves 6–8

I make these for a church festival every year, and they sell out early! Leftover couscous? Try couscous cakes (separate recipe).

Serving Idea

Try creamy cucumber sauce or pomegranate-pepper preserves (separate recipes).

Ingredients

1 lb. ground beef or ground lamb (or ½ lb. of each)

1 cup cooked and cooled couscous

¼ cup toasted pine nuts

3 scallions, chopped finely

3 cloves fresh garlic, minced

1 large egg, beaten

¼ cup chopped parsley, preferably flat-leaf

1 tbsp. olive oil

1 tbsp. dried mint, or 3 tbsp. fresh mint

1 tbsp. dried marjoram or oregano

½ tsp. cinnamon

Optional: 2–3 oz. Feta cheese, crumbled

2 tsp. lemon zest

1–2 tsp. kosher salt

½ tsp. paprika, preferably smoked paprika

Optional: 24 oz. prepared marinara sauce

Additional 1–2 tbsp. olive oil, for frying

Directions

Mix ingredients through paprika. Form into about 15 meatballs, made egg-shaped for a change, if you like. Flatten slightly if making sliders. Refrigerate at least one hour, to let flavors blend.

For meatballs, preheat oven to 400 degrees. Bake meatballs on a parchment-lined cookie sheet for 25–30 minutes, until surfaces start to brown. After baking, drop meatballs into hot marinara sauce on stovetop. Cover and cook for about 15 minutes on medium-low heat, until meat is cooked through and flavors have combined, spooning sauce over the meatballs as they simmer.

For sliders, skip baking step. Heat a large nonstick skillet or nonstick stovetop grill over medium heat. Coat sliders with nonstick spray. Cook well, turning once, about 6 minutes total.

Chicken Mornay

8 servings

Duke Philippe De Mornay (1549–1623), a French Huguenot leader, invented béchamel sauce. Béchamel sauce is a variation of the basic white sauce of Mornay. Today, Mornay is a small village in the region of Bourgogne in central/eastern France.

Ingredients

2 lb. boneless, skinless chicken breasts

⅓ cup flour, seasoned with 2 tsp. salt and 1 tsp. pepper

3 tbsp. butter, regular or light, divided

1 tbsp. olive oil

12 oz. mushrooms, sliced

1 tsp. dried thyme

Zest and juice of 1 lemon, divided (about 2 tbsp. juice and 2 tsp. zest)

1¼ cups prepared Bechamel sauce (separate recipe, make ½ batch)

½ cup low-sodium chicken broth

4 oz. thinly sliced or grated Swiss or similar cheese such as Jarlsberg

Optional: chopped parsley for garnish

Optional: serve with fresh peaches (traditional) or apricot pepper preserves (separate recipe)

Directions

Dredge chicken breasts in seasoned flour. Heat a large sauté pan on medium heat. Add 1 tbsp. butter and 1 tbsp. olive oil. Cook breasts 5 minutes per side, or until cooked through. Remove to a baking dish that's been coated with nonstick spray.

In same pan, continuing on medium heat, sauté mushrooms, thyme, and lemon zest in remaining 2 tbsp. butter, until mushrooms are cooked and releasing liquid. Add Bechamel sauce along with chicken broth and lemon juice. Bring to a boil; reduce heat to low and simmer 10 minutes.

Pour sauce over chicken. Top with cheese. Cover and bake at 350 degrees for 20 minutes. Uncover and bake 8–12 minutes more, until hot and bubbly.

Pecan-Crusted Chicken

6 servings

Serving Idea

Serve with mashed potatoes. Leftovers? Slice and serve over a baby spinach or kale salad, with sliced pears and blue or goat cheese.

Pecans are a good source of iron, calcium, copper, manganese, and fiber.

Marinade

½ cup buttermilk
1 tbsp. Dijon mustard

2 cloves minced garlic
1 tsp. hot sauce

Chicken

1½ lb. skinless, boneless chicken breasts,
   pounded to about ½ inch
1 cup finely chopped pecans
¼ cup panko breadcrumbs
1 tsp. dried rosemary, crushed to release flavor

1 tsp. kosher salt
½ tsp. black pepper
About 2 tbsp. olive oil and 2 tbsp. butter (for
   pan-frying)

Directions

Put chicken in a gallon Ziploc bag. Mix marinade ingredients. Pour over chicken; marinate in refrigerator for 30–60 minutes. Drain. Discard marinade.

Meanwhile, combine ingredients through pepper in a wide, flat bowl. Press onto both sides of chicken. Sauté in 1 tbsp. olive oil and 1 tbsp. butter over medium heat, about 5 minutes per side, until no longer pink in center. If meat isn't fully cooked, finish by baking at 350 degrees for 8–10 minutes.

Roast Pork Tenderloin with Spanish Almond Topping

4 servings

Almonds are high in protein. They are helpful in lowering blood pressure, and they have heart-healthy properties. This dish is topped with pomegranate sauce. Pomegranates are a good source of vitamin C and potassium, and they have cholesterol-fighting properties.

Symbolically, pomegranates represent perennial fertility and immortality. In Christianity, the seeds are said to represent the members of the church, bound together as one.

You may have extra crumbs. They will keep for at least a week. Try them on pan-roasted fish or roasted veggies.

Ingredients

2 tbsp. olive oil

¾ cup sliced almonds

3 garlic cloves, minced

¾ cup panko breadcrumbs

2 tsp. dried rosemary, crushed to release flavor

1 tsp. smoked paprika

Salt and pepper to taste

1 lb. pork tenderloin

Pomegranate sauce with cherries (separate recipe)

Directions

Preheat oven to 425 degrees, with rack in middle of oven.

Heat oil in a large heavy skillet over medium heat until it shimmers. Add almonds; sauté until pale golden, about 30 seconds. Stir in garlic; cook 1 minute. Add panko, rosemary, 1 tsp. paprika, ½ tsp. salt, and ½ tsp. pepper.

Turn down heat to medium-low; cook 2–3 minutes, until very fragrant. Cool slightly, then chop finely in a food processor. Transfer to a large plate.

Roll pork in crumbs. Place on a foil- or parchment-lined baking sheet. Cover with foil. Roast until an instant-read thermometer registers 145–150°F, about 25 minutes. Let stand 10 minutes before slicing.

Favorites from the South and Southwest

Rather Tasty Barbeque Brisket

12–15 servings

This recipe is based loosely on newscaster Dan Rather's recipe, which was published many years ago in the *Houston Chronicle*. His method is low and slow in the oven. I mostly prefer the crockpot.

The oven method is somewhat better suited to slices; the crockpot is better for chunks. In either case, be prepared to start the day before you serve. It takes time—but not too much effort. It's worth it!

According to their website, Colgin Liquid Smoke is all-natural, and vegan—although one wonders how relevant that is if you're slathering it on a big hunk of brisket. The company was started in 1938.

For a Tex-Mex variation, use red chile-pepita sauce (separate recipe) on the last step instead of BBQ sauce.

Ingredients

1 4–5 lb. trimmed beef brisket

1 3-oz. bottle liquid smoke (such as Texas-based Colgin)

Rub: 1 tsp. celery salt or celery seed, 1 tsp. garlic salt, 2 tsp. lemon pepper, and 2 tsp. onion powder

12 oz. of your favorite beer, preferably full-bodied

½ cup Worcestershire sauce

16 oz. prepared barbecue sauce

Oven Method: Day One

Line a roasting pan with heavy-duty foil, using 2 sheets if necessary to enclose brisket. Poke brisket in multiple places using a large fork. Place beef on foil. Sprinkle half the Liquid Smoke on top, then half the rub mixture and half the beer. Turn the meat over and repeat. Wrap tightly; crimp foil to create a seal. Refrigerate overnight.

Day Two

Open the packet, season with Worcestershire sauce; reseal. If one side has more fat, put that side up. Cook in a 250-degree oven for 5 hours. Remove meat from oven and unwrap, leaving a foil collar. Spread the top of the meat with about half the barbecue sauce.

Increase oven temperature to 300 degrees. Bake the brisket uncovered for a final hour. To test tenderness, poke with a small knife in several places. If meat resists—if the knife doesn't cut through easily—cook another 30 minutes or longer.

Let sit at least 15 minutes after removing from oven. Adjust seasonings. Slice across the grain and serve with more barbecue sauce.

Crockpot Method: Day One

Mix together rub ingredients. Set aside. Place beef in crockpot. Poke brisket in multiple places using a large fork. Sprinkle half the liquid smoke on top, then half the rub mixture and half the beer. Turn the meat over and repeat. Refrigerate overnight. Or do this in the morning of day one and cook per directions below, overnight.

Day Two

Season the meat with Worcestershire sauce on both sides. If one side has more fat, put that side up. Cook on high 7–9 hours, until very tender. Stir in all the barbeque sauce. Continue heating 1 more hour, uncovered. If possible, let the meat continue to sit in the powered-off crockpot another 30–60 minutes, to absorb more barbeque flavor. Adjust seasonings, adding salt and pepper if desired.

Eggs Sardou

4 servings

A Louisiana classic! Created by Antoine's, one of New Orleans' grand old-line restaurants.

Traditionally, artichoke bottoms serve as the base of this dish. I have found that it's easier to purchase quartered hearts.

So I make a base of an English muffin or corn cake (separate recipe), then add spinach, quartered artichoke hearts, eggs, and Hollandaise. You can even dollop pesto on top if you like.

Eggs are an excellent source of protein. Spinach is a good source of beta-carotene, potassium, vitamin C, and vitamin K, and it is heart-healthy and enhances memory. The creamed spinach and hollandaise can be made in a calorie-saving manner.

Ingredients

Base: 4 English muffins, halved and toasted; or 8 corn cakes; or 8 cooked artichoke bottoms
For muffins: 4 tbsp. butter—regular or light—softened
1 cup creamed spinach (separate recipe)

1 can quartered artichokes, drained and rinsed
8 poached eggs*
1 cup hollandaise sauce (separate recipe)
Dash of paprika, preferably smoked paprika
Salt and black pepper to taste

Directions

Butter toasted muffins if using. Top each base with creamed spinach, quartered artichokes and poached eggs, then drizzle with hollandaise.

*If you don't have a microwave or stovetop egg poacher, you can use a skillet and white vinegar. Pour water in saucepan to 2–3 inches. Add 3–4 tbsp. white vinegar, depending on size of skillet. Add 1 tsp. kosher salt. Bring to a boil; slide in eggs one at a time. Immediately turn off heat, cover, and let sit until done, 3–4 minutes. Remove with a slotted spoon.

Southwestern Pimiento Cheese

Makes about 2½ cups

Can be made with light mayonnaise and light butter. Try different cheeses, to your taste; the recipe is very flexible.

Serving Ideas

Serve on crackers or bruschetta, topped if desired with halved grape tomatoes; or use as filling for celery. Sandwich: try making a grilled pimiento cheese sandwich with thinly sliced tomato, and thinly sliced deli ham if desired.

Ingredients

4 garlic cloves, freshly minced if possible

¼ cup diced roasted red bell peppers and 2 tbsp. juice from jar

1 shallot, diced

2 tbsp. chopped fresh or pickled jalapenos, along with 1 tbsp. brine if desired

3 cups (12 oz.) coarsely grated sharp cheddar or a combination of cheddar and a white cheese

¼ cup mayonnaise — regular or light

¼ cup butter—regular or light— softened

Dash cayenne or smoked paprika

Directions

In a large bowl, combine all ingredients except cayenne. Stir well. Season to taste with cayenne or paprika. Cheese spread may be made several days ahead and chilled, covered. Bring spread to room temperature before serving.

Pimiento Mac and Cheese

Add 3 tbsp. sour cream and 4 oz. cooked pasta to each 1 cup prepared pimiento cheese. Combine well. Add topping: ½ cup chopped tomato, ¼ cup lightly toasted pine nuts (optional), and ¼ cup finely grated Parmesan cheese. Sprinkle with black pepper or paprika. Bake at 350 degrees till bubbly, about 30 minutes.

Sweet and Spicy Pecans

Makes 4 cups

Another New Orleans favorite! Can be eaten out of hand or added to salads. See recipe below for spicy pecan bacon.

 A pecan is a type of hickory nut that is native to South America. Pecans have grown wild in Texas since Cabeza de Vaca spotted them in the sixteenth century. The name "pecan" derives from an Algonquin Indian word meaning "a nut too hard to crack by hand." Definitely worth buying already-shelled nuts.

Ingredients

4 cups pecan halves (1 lb.)
1 stick (½ cup) unsalted butter
½ cup granulated sugar

2 tsp. salt
½-1 tsp. cayenne

Directions

Preheat oven to 325 degrees. Place pecans in a medium mixing bowl. Melt butter, using a microwave if you like. Pour butter over nuts and mix well. In a small bowl, whisk together remaining ingredients. Sprinkle over pecans and mix well.

Spread in a single layer on a rimmed cookie sheet lined with parchment paper or non-stick foil. Bake until lightly toasted, 14–15 minutes.

Spicy Pecan Bacon

To save time, rather than preparing sweet and spicy pecans, you can make bacon topping by processing ½ cup fresh pecans, 1 tbsp. sugar, 1 tbsp. maple syrup, and a dash of cayenne and salt. Preheat oven or toaster oven to 375 degrees. Pulse ½ cup prepared pecans and 1 tbsp. maple syrup in small food processor, until mixture reaches a fine consistency. Place 6–8 strips bacon on a foil- or parchment-lined pan. Sprinkle with chopped pecans. Bake until done, 10–15 minutes. Drizzle with additional maple syrup if desired. Cut into bite-sized pieces or serve strips with steak.

Shrimp and Grits

4 main-dish servings or 8 appetizer servings

You can serve over grits or corn cakes (separate recipes). Corn cakes can be made small for appetizer-size servings. Prefer rice? Make "shrimp-y" rice by using shrimp broth instead of water as you boil rice according to package directions. For a Southwestern flair, serve with a little green salsa.

In the Lowcountry of South Carolina, particularly Charleston, shrimp and grits has been around for many decades, as a basic breakfast for coastal fishermen. Simply called breakfast shrimp, the dish originally consisted of a pot of grits with shrimp cooked in a little bacon grease or butter.

Ingredients

1 lb. fresh or frozen raw shrimp in shell, preferably large or extra-large

1 tsp. Old Bay seasoning

1 stick (½ cup) butter—regular or light

½ cup dry white wine

1 cup shrimp broth, seafood broth, or clam juice (note that directions below make shrimp broth)

2 tbsp. minced shallots or sweet onion

4 cloves freshly minced garlic

2 tbsp. chopped or julienned sun-dried tomatoes packed in oil, drained

Zest and juice of 1 lemon

1 tsp. Worcestershire sauce

2 tbsp. minced parsley

Creole seasoning or salt and pepper to taste; or try Sriracha sauce

Gorgonzola grits or corn cakes, prepared (separate recipes)

Directions

For shrimp broth, bring 5 cups water and 1 tsp. Old Bay seasoning to a boil over high heat in a medium saucepan. Add uncooked shrimp in their shells. Lower heat to medium. If fresh, cook just 1–2 minutes; if frozen, cook 3–5 minutes, until no longer translucent. Don't overcook. Using a slotted spoon, remove shrimp to a bowl of ice water, reserving broth. Keep simmering the cooking water while you peel shrimp, to concentrate its flavor. Add shells to broth. Refrigerate shelled shrimp until ready to use.

Boil stock and shells for 10 minutes; strain, reserving 1 cup for this recipe and 3 cups total if making grits (grits recipe requires 2 cups.)

Melt butter over medium heat. Add wine, 1 cup broth, and shallots. Cook, stirring often, until mixture is reduced somewhat, about 5–6 minutes. Turn down heat to low. Add ingredients through Worcestershire sauce; simmer 10 minutes. Add cooked shrimp and parsley; cook over low heat just until heated through. Adjust seasonings.

Seafood Gumbo

Serves 8–10

This recipe has lots of ingredients, but it's worth the effort, for the layers of flavor. The fragrance is wonderful! And it contains lots of veggies.

The name "gumbo" comes from a West African word for okra. The use of filé (dried sassafras leaves) came from the Choctaws. In 1803, gumbo was served at a gubernatorial reception in New Orleans, and in 1804 gumbo was served at a Cajun gathering on the Acadian Coast. "Cajun" is short for Acadian, and denotes a group of people who migrated to southern Louisiana from Nova Scotia and nearby areas, beginning in the eighteenth century.

Shrimp Sauté Mixture and Stock Ingredients

2 lb. raw medium or large shrimp, shell-on

1 tsp. garlic salt

2 tsp. garlic powder

2 tsp. dried thyme

¼–½ tsp. cayenne pepper

2 tbsp. fish sauce, found in the Asian section of well-stocked groceries

4 cups water—for making shrimp stock—to yield 2 cups concentrated stock

1 tsp. Old Bay seasoning

Juice of ½ lemon

2 tbsp. vegetable oil, for sautéing shrimp

Shrimp Preparation

Remove shells from shrimp, saving shells. Toss shelled shrimp with salt, garlic powder, thyme, and pepper; stir in fish sauce. Allow to sit for 10 minutes. Meanwhile, prepare broth. Heat water, Old Bay, lemon juice, and shrimp shells in a saucepan over high heat, until boiling. Reduce heat to medium-low and simmer while you continue with the recipe.

Heat oil in a Dutch oven over medium heat. Add seasoned shrimp and cook, stirring often, until shrimp are opaque, 4–5 minutes. Be careful not to overcook. Remove from heat.

Refrigerate shrimp; drain the "juice," reserving it. Turn off heat under shrimp shells. Strain the shells; save broth for step below. Discard shells.

Roux and Vegetable Mixture

2 cups chopped sweet onion

1 cup chopped celery with leaves

1 cup chopped poblano pepper or green bell pepper

2 cups chopped okra; frozen works well

½ cup vegetable oil

½ cup flour

2 bay leaves

12 oz. mild-flavored beer

1 tbsp. Worcestershire sauce or Pickapeppa sauce

1 14-oz. can diced tomatoes in juice, undrained

Optional: ⅓ cup chopped green onions, including tops

2 lb. sautéed shrimp—from above

8–12 oz. crabmeat (use 12 oz. if you aren't adding oysters)

Optional: 8 oz. oysters

Optional: gumbo filé, for sprinkling

Directions

In a medium bowl, combine onion, celery, and poblano pepper. Stir in okra.

In Dutch oven, heat oil over medium heat until it ripples. Carefully add flour, and whisk to combine. Stirring often, heat the roux until it's the color of milk chocolate, and somewhat thickened, about 15 minutes. You may think the mixture is burning—it may start to smell like overcooked popcorn—but persevere! Your olfactory senses will be rewarded in the next step.

Turn off heat. Very carefully add vegetable mixture to hot roux; stir to combine. Add bay leaves. Add 2 cups shrimp stock, beer, Worcestershire sauce, tomatoes, and "juice" from the sautéed shrimp. Bring to a boil over medium heat; reduce heat to medium-low and simmer 15 minutes.

Add green onions and seafood; gently simmer until warm throughout. Sprinkle with filé before serving.

Cajun Red Beans and Rice

6–8 servings

The Acadia region from where the Cajuns emigrated consisted largely of what are now Nova Scotia and the other Maritime provinces of Canada, plus parts of eastern Quebec and northern Maine. Since some Cajuns came from Louisiana to East Texas after the "Second Spindletop" oil discovery in the early 1920s, you'll find Cajun cuisine in both states.

Red beans are a good source of fiber and low-fat protein. The fiber, folate, and magnesium lower heart attack risk and help regulate blood sugar.

Ingredients

1 tbsp. olive oil

1 lb. smoked sausage, cut in ½-inch slices

1 small sweet onion, chopped: about 1¼ cups

2 stalks celery, with leaves, chopped

1 medium green bell or poblano pepper, chopped

2 15-oz. cans red kidney beans, preferably low-sodium, undrained

12 oz. beer

1 tsp. kosher salt—more to taste

1½ tsp. thyme

1½ tsp. marjoram or oregano

1½ tsp. garlic powder

½ tsp. cayenne pepper—more to taste

1 large or 2 small bay leaves

Optional: grated cheddar cheese and chopped green onions, for topping

Directions

Heat oil in a Dutch oven over medium heat. Add sausage. Cook, stirring often, until sausage begins to brown.

Add onions, celery, and bell pepper. Sauté 6–8 minutes, until veggies are soft. Add beans, undrained, plus remaining ingredients through bay leaves. Stir only until combined.

Bring to a boil. Reduce heat to low, cover, and simmer 30 minutes. Remove bay leaves. Garnish with shredded cheddar cheese and chopped green onion. Serve over rice.

Beer-Braised Greens

4–6 servings

Greens are very nutritious, and they contain vitamins A, C, and K, manganese, fiber, calcium, and more! Try this recipe using turnip, collard, mustard, or kale greens.

My friend Phyllis and her mother Hazel are from Florida, and they remind me that in the South, greens are traditionally cooked longer than called for here. Cook to your taste.

Ingredients

2 tbsp. bacon grease

4–6 slices bacon

1–2 turnip bottoms, peeled and cubed into ½ inch cubes (or use chopped rutabaga, red potato, or sweet potato, or ½ medium onion, preferably sweet onion, chopped or thinly sliced)

1 large bunch greens, rinsed and coarsely chopped, tough stems removed

12 oz. light-flavored beer

½ tsp. black pepper

½ tsp. salt

4 garlic cloves, minced

1½ tbsp. cider vinegar or red wine vinegar (cider vinegar works well if you're including sweet potatoes)

Optional: hot sauce or pepper sauce to taste

Optional: dash sugar or 1–2 tbsp. maple syrup (if greens taste bitter)

Directions

Cut bacon into ½- to 1-inch pieces. Add to a cold Dutch oven. Turn heat to medium. Cook bacon, stirring often, until just crisp. Remove pieces with a slotted spoon; set aside.

Add turnip or onion; stir until coated with grease. Add greens, beer, salt, pepper, and garlic; bring to a boil. Cover loosely, reduce heat to medium-low, and simmer 30–45 minutes, stirring occasionally, until tender. Remove lid, add the bacon bits again, and stir until most liquid is evaporated, about 5 minutes. Stir in vinegar and optional hot sauce.

Fried Green Tomatoes

6–10 servings

Salad

Serve over a bed of arugula, baby spinach, or baby kale with ranch dressing or creamy cucumber dressing. Try Sriracha aioli, chili-lime, or remoulade sauces. Add a sprinkling of pan-roasted almonds or pecans for extra crunch and flavor. Be sure to use unripe tomatoes because ripe ones won't hold the coating (as noted below).

 Fried green tomatoes aren't exclusively Southern.

> Lovers of tomatoes are very fond of them, sliced green as apples are sliced, and fried in butter. Some persons are fond of them sliced and fried after being dipped in butter. The green tomatoes, which the season will not permit to ripen, may be turned to good account by using them fried.
> —*The New England Farmer,* October 14, 1836

Ingredients

4 large unripe tomatoes, ends removed, cut into ¼- to ½-inch thick slices

1½ cups buttermilk

½ cup all-purpose flour—more to taste

1 tsp. garlic salt—more to taste

Several pinches cayenne pepper

1 cup cornmeal—more to taste

2 beaten eggs

⅓ cup olive oil—more as needed

Directions

Put sliced tomatoes in a gallon Ziploc bag. Pour buttermilk over tomato slices; let sit 15 minutes at room temperature, gently shaking several times to coat.

Meanwhile, in a shallow bowl, combine half the flour, half the garlic salt, and a pinch of cayenne. Put half the cornmeal in another dish. Put the eggs in another shallow dish, so you have an assembly line for the three coatings.

Shake excess buttermilk from tomatoes, dust with seasoned flour, dip in beaten eggs, and then dredge in cornmeal mixture, coating well and shaking off excess. Refresh coatings as necessary.

Place a large heavy skillet or griddle over medium heat and coat with 2–3 tbsp. of oil. When oil is hot, pan-fry tomatoes, in batches, until golden brown and crispy on both sides, 2½–3 minutes on first side, until starting to brown, and 2–2½ minutes on second side. Add oil as necessary. Carefully remove the tomatoes and drain on paper towels. Serve with choice of sauces.

To reheat, heat at 350 degrees for about 8–10 minutes.

Red Chile-Pepita Sauce

About 1¼ cups sauce

Try with grilled chicken, or Rather Tasty BBQ brisket. Also good with burgers. Try making red chile chili - directions following recipe.

Ingredients

6 large (about 5–7 inches) dried red chiles such as guajillo

3 cups water

2 tsp. ground cumin

2 tbsp. olive or vegetable oil

1 small onion, coarsely chopped (about 1 cup)

5 cloves garlic, sliced or minced

½ cup tamarind juice, nectar, or soda*

1 tablespoon lime juice

6 oz. mild-flavored beer or 3 oz. dry white wine

⅓ cup roasted and salted pepitas (hulled pumpkin seeds)

1 teaspoon dried marjoram or oregano

1 cup canned fire-roasted tomatoes, including juice

Salt and cayenne or black pepper to taste

Directions

Bring water to a boil. Meanwhile, rinse chiles. Submerge chiles in boiling water. Turn off heat; cover. Let soak for 30 minutes. Remove stems, seeds, and cores, and tear into 1-inch wide strips. Save 1 cup soaking water.

Heat a large heavy skillet over medium heat. Toast cumin 1–2 minutes, stirring constantly, until fragrant. Add oil. Add hydrated ancho pieces, onion, and garlic. Reduce heat to medium-low. Sauté 5 minutes, stirring often.

Add tamarind juice, lime juice, beer, pepitas, marjoram, and tomatoes. Increase heat to medium. Bring mixture to a boil, then reduce heat to a simmer, cover, and cook 20 minutes, stirring several times.

Puree with a handheld immersion blender (or let cool a bit and use a food processor). Add water if necessary to thin out texture. Season to taste with salt and cayenne or black pepper.

*You may find cans of tamarind nectar, such as Jumex brand, in the grocery. If you can't find tamarind beverages, try using 2 tsp. tamarind paste and ½ cup water. If you can't find any tamarind products, use 2 tsp. honey (more to taste) and ½ cup water. Increase the lime juice to 2 tbsp.

Red chile chili

1 lb. ground beef, preferably 80/20
1 tbsp. chili powder
1 tsp. garlic powder
2 tsp. cumin
¼ cup ketchup
1 cup prepared red chile-pepita sauce (above)

½ cup water
12 oz. Sofrito (such as Goya brand: tomato-flavored cooking base, sold in a jar)
Optional: 1 can low-sodium pinto beans, undrained

Cook beef over medium heat until no longer pink. Drain if desired. Add ingredients through ketchup; reduce to medium-low, simmer 5 minutes. Add remaining ingredients. Simmer 20 minutes.

Fire-Roasted Tomato Salsa

Makes about 1½ cups

See Spanish rice and Tex-Mex meatloaf recipes for two tasty ways to use this salsa, in addition to a dip for tortilla chips.

Ingredients

1 15-oz. can fire-roasted diced tomatoes, drained

5 cloves garlic, peeled

2 green onions, chopped (or ¼ medium red onion)

½ tsp. cumin—more to taste

1 medium poblano pepper (or 2–3 jalapenos, seeded and chopped)

2 tbsp. lime juice

1 tbsp. olive oil

Optional: ¼ cup chopped cilantro—more to taste

Optional: 1–2 pinches sugar

Salt and pepper to taste

Directions

In a food processor, combine ingredients through cilantro. For a chunkier texture, chop by hand and stir together. Taste; add sugar, salt, and pepper to taste. Store in refrigerator.

Green Salsa

Makes about 4 cups

Serving Ideas

For tacos, enchiladas, pulled pork, pork stew, Tex-Mex meatloaf, and, naturally, chips!

Creamy Green Salsa with Avocado

Add 1 avocado and 1 tbsp. lime juice to ½ cup salsa.

Tomatillos are a good source of vitamin C, fiber, and potassium.

Ingredients

2 tbsp. olive oil

1 large onion—preferably sweet onion—coarsely chopped

5–6 cloves peeled garlic, whole or minced

1½ lb. tomatillos, husked and quartered or halved (depending on size)

1 tsp. kosher salt—more to taste

2 large poblano peppers, roasted (about 30 minutes at 400 degrees) then seeded, peeled, and coarsely chopped

3 cups low-sodium chicken broth

1½ tsp. cumin

½ tsp. black pepper

Optional: ½ bunch cilantro, coarsely chopped (or 2 tbsp. coriander/cilantro chutney)

Optional: 1–2 tbsp. sugar (if mixture tastes sour) or 1–2 tbsp. sour cream or Greek yogurt (if too spicy)

Directions

In a Dutch oven or stockpot, heat olive oil over medium heat. Sauté onion, garlic, tomatillos, and salt until onion is translucent, 6–8 minutes.

Add roasted peppers, chicken broth, cumin, and black pepper. Bring to a boil. Add cilantro, reduce heat to medium-low, cover loosely, and simmer 30 minutes. Use an immersion blender to blend. Add a little sugar if mixture tastes sour. If it's too spicy, add 1–2 tbsp. plain Greek yogurt or sour cream. Reduce heat to medium-low; simmer uncovered until thickened, 20–30 minutes.

Mango Salsa

Makes about 3 cups

Mangoes are a very good source of vitamins A and C, magnesium, and fiber.

Serving Ideas

Topping for white-flesh fish (including fish tacos), salmon, crab cakes, or over Brie.

Ingredients

2 ripe mangoes, peeled and diced
½ cup diced red onion
1 jalapeno, seeded and minced
2 tbsp. fresh orange juice
2 tbsp. fresh lime juice

¼ cup minced red bell pepper
Pinch salt
Optional: 1 tbsp. Curacao or other orange liqueur
Optional: 1–2 tsp. hot sauce

Directions

Combine all ingredients. Chill until ready to use.

Skirt Steak with a Cayenne Kick

6 servings

This can be made on an indoor or outdoor grill. Or use a heavy skillet.

Serving Ideas

Make into tacos, with shredded lettuce or cabbage tossed with salsa, chimichurri sauce, or chili-lime sauce (separate recipes) or make a steak salad with a vinaigrette dressing, adding your favorite cheese.

Ingredients

1½ lb. skirt steak, cut into 2 pieces if necessary to fit pan
¼ cup dry sherry
2 tbsp. lime juice
2 tbsp. soy sauce

Optional: 1 tbsp. Asian fish sauce (for another layer of flavor)
2 tsp. sugar (to increase "char")
Cayenne butter sauce (see below)

Directions

Use a meat mallet to pound steak on both sides, in order to tenderize this very lean cut. If you don't have a mallet, use a heavy pan. Place in Ziploc bag. Sprinkle with sherry, lime juice, soy sauce, and fish sauce. Marinate in refrigerator 15 minutes. Wipe off sherry mixture with paper towel. Sprinkle with sugar. Meanwhile, heat grill over medium heat for 5 minutes.

Grill steak about 3 minutes per side. Remove from heat. While still hot, coat with butter mixture, recipe below. Let steak cool for about 10 minutes; cut against the grain.

Cayenne Butter Sauce for Skirt Steak

3 tbsp. butter, softened
1 tbsp. honey

¼–½ tsp. cayenne pepper, to taste
1 tsp. onion salt

In small bowl, combine ingredients with a fork. Set aside.

Tex-Mex Meatloaf

6 servings

This meatloaf has a bold Mexican flavor and is easy to make.

Incorporate homemade red or green salsa if you like. Serve with Spanish rice and charro beans (separate recipes). Add a green salad with orange-avocado dressing to complete the meal.

Ingredients

1½ lb. ground beef (preferably 80/20)
1 small onion, chopped
1 medium poblano pepper, chopped
1 large egg
Optional: ⅓ cup minced cilantro or 1 tbsp. coriander chutney or cilantro chutney
¾ cup coarsely crushed tortilla chips or corn chips

1 package taco seasoning (or 1 heaping tbsp. chili powder, 1 tsp. garlic powder, and 1 tsp. cumin)
Salt and pepper to taste
1 cup shredded cheddar cheese, divided
⅔ cup green or red salsa, store-bought or homemade (separate recipes), divided
Optional: sour cream, for serving

Directions

Mix thoroughly ingredients through salt and pepper. Stir in half the cheese, then half the salsa. Shape into loaf and put into loaf pan. Spread remaining salsa over top of loaf. Put into oven preheated to 350 degrees and bake for 45 minutes. Put remaining cheese on top of loaf and continue baking for 15–20 minutes.

Blackened Grilled Shrimp Tacos

4 servings

Serving Ideas

Serve with mango salsa, green or red salsa, chili-lime sauce; Sriracha aioli (separate recipes). Many corn tortillas have only about 50 calories per tortilla, making this recipe calorie-wise.

Spice Mixture

1 tsp. paprika, preferably smoked paprika
1 heaping tsp. ground cumin
1 tsp. garlic powder
1 tsp. dried marjoram or oregano

1 tsp. kosher salt
1 tsp. dried thyme
¼ tsp. cayenne pepper

Shrimp

1 lb. medium shrimp, peeled and deveined
2 tbsp. olive or vegetable oil

2 tbsp. lime or lemon juice

Tacos and Toppings

8 corn tortillas or tostada shells
½ cup diced tomato
1 ripe avocado, sliced thinly

2 oz. queso fresco or Cotija cheese, crumbled
  (about ½ cup)
Shredded lettuce or cabbage
Juice of 1 lime

Directions

Combine spice ingredients in a small bowl. Set aside. Place shrimp in a quart-sized Ziploc bag. Pour in the olive oil and lime juice; coat well. Add spice mixture; shake to combine well. Marinate 10 minutes in refrigerator. Remove shrimp; discard marinade. Thread shrimp onto skewers if desired.

Heat a grill pan over medium-high heat for several minutes. Add shrimp; cook 2 minutes per side or until done. Sprinkle with lime juice. Fill tortillas; add desired toppings.

Divide shrimp evenly among tortillas. Add toppings as desired. Sprinkle with lime juice. Drizzle with sauce of your choice.

Crockpot Southwestern Pulled Pork

8–10 servings

I find the combination of orange juice, lime juice, and cumin to be distinctive and quite tasty—without adding too much heat. Assembling this dish is quick—and then let the crockpot do the work.

Serving Ideas

Serve with shredded cabbage in corn tortillas, and top with red or green salsa, chopped cilantro, and avocado if desired. Or serve with corn cakes instead of tortillas. Try with a side of Spanish rice and black beans.

Ingredients

2½–3 lb. boneless pork roast, preferably pork loin
2 tsp. kosher salt
1 tsp. black pepper
1½ tbsp. olive oil
5 cloves garlic, peeled

1 tbsp. cumin
1 tsp. marjoram or oregano
1½ cups freshly squeezed orange juice, from 6–8 "juice" oranges such as Valencia
⅓ cup lime juice, from 4–6 limes

Rub pork with salt and pepper. Heat oil in a Dutch oven over medium-high heat. Add pork and brown on all sides, 6 to 8 minutes. Transfer to a crockpot.

Combine remaining ingredients in a small food processor. Blend well. Pour liquid over pork in crockpot. Cook on high for 3–4 hours or on low for 7–8 hours, until very tender. Remove pork and shred with a fork. Add pork back to pot. Cook another 30 minutes to fully blend flavors.

Tex-Mex Charro Beans

Serves 6–8

Heart-healthy pinto beans are a good source of folate, fiber, manganese, magnesium, potassium, iron, and protein.

The origins of *frijoles charros* are found in the Mexican cowboys who would work long days herding cattle. The dish called for dried beans. This dish could be left to cook for many hours in a Dutch oven. The early recipes called for many dried or preserved ingredients so they could be carried and stored for extended periods without going bad, and they could stand up to long cooking times.

Serving Idea

Leftover beans can be mashed or blended into a paste for a dip; add sour cream, lime juice, and hot sauce to taste. For a hot dip, top with cheddar cheese and serve in a small crockpot.

Ingredients

6–8 strips bacon, and 1–2 tbsp. bacon grease

3 cloves garlic, minced

1 small onion, chopped (about 1 cup)

2 jalapeno peppers (seeded and chopped) or ¼ cup chopped pickled jalapeno

2 cans reduced-sodium pinto beans, undrained

Optional: ½–1 tsp. cumin

12 oz. light-flavored beer

Optional: ⅓ cup chopped fresh cilantro or 2 tsp. coriander/cilantro chutney

Salt and pepper to taste

Directions

Place bacon in a cold Dutch oven. Cook until crispy over medium heat. Remove bacon; chop when cooled. Reserve 2 tbsp. bacon grease; discard remainder. Add garlic, onions, and jalapeno to Dutch oven; cook over medium heat until onions are translucent, 5–7 minutes. Add bacon bits.

Add beer to bacon mixture and simmer a few additional minutes, until liquid is reduced by about a third. Add beans with their liquid (plus optional cumin), bring to a boil, and then reduce heat and simmer about 10 minutes. Add chopped cilantro, salt, and pepper to taste.

Spanish Rice

4–6 servings

Thanks to my friend Rebecca for the soup mix idea! See note below.

Ingredients

2 tbsp. olive oil

¼ cup minced shallot or onion

1 cup uncooked white rice

2½ cups chicken broth*

⅔ cup high-quality red salsa (or use separate recipe for tomato salsa)*

Optional: 1 tsp. cumin

Directions

Heat oil in a large, heavy skillet over medium heat. Stir in onion, and cook 1 minute. Add rice; cook 5 minutes, stirring often.

When rice begins to brown, stir in chicken broth and salsa. Or see soup directions below. Bring to a boil. Reduce heat to low, so that rice is barely boiling, cover loosely and simmer 18–20 minutes, until liquid has been absorbed, checking at 15 minutes to make sure there's enough liquid. Add cumin if desired. Cumin will make the recipe "pop." Fluff with a fork and serve.

*Alternative preparation

For a subtler flavor, eliminate salsa. Use a packaged dry tomato soup mix, such as Goya Sazon with cilantro and tomato (use 3 cups chicken broth with 2 packets of a 1.4-oz. box). You can also use 2 Knorr Caldo de Tomate cubes from an 8-cube box, mixed with 3 cups hot water instead of chicken broth, since the cubes have chicken flavor.) Add cumin if desired.

Tres Leches (Three Milks Cake)

About 12 servings

The idea of creating a cake soaked in liquid most likely originated in medieval Europe: tres leches is similar to the British trifle and Italian tiramisu. Recipes for soaked-cake desserts existed in Mexico as early as the 1800s, possibly because of cultural and trade ties between Europe and the Americas. Recipes for tres leches appeared on Nestlé condensed milk can labels in the 1940s.

For color, texture, and additional flavor, I like to add toppings like berries, peaches, mangoes, caramel sauce, or toasted coconut.

Cake

6 large eggs, separated, plus 1 tsp. white vinegar,
    to keep egg whites stiff
2 cups granulated sugar
2 tsp. vanilla extract
2 cups all-purpose flour

1 tsp. kosher salt
2 tsp. baking powder
½ cup evaporated milk from a 12-oz. can (use
    remainder of can for topping)

Cream Topping

1 cup heavy whipping cream (use another cup for frosting)
1 cup evaporated milk

1 14–oz. can sweetened condensed milk
Optional: ¼ cup Grand Marnier, Curacao, or limoncello liqueur

Frosting

1 cup heavy whipping cream
¼ cup powdered sugar

½ tsp. vanilla extract

Cake

Preheat the oven to 350 degrees. Grease and flour a 9x13 baking dish; set aside. In mixer bowl, beat egg whites several minutes on high speed until soft peaks form. Add vinegar; continue to beat to form stiff peaks. Beat in sugar, mixing on medium speed for 2 minutes. Add egg yolks one at a time, then vanilla, beating well on medium speed to incorporate. In separate bowl, whisk together flour, salt, and baking powder. Add to egg mixture, alternating with milk. Beat 2 minutes. Pour into prepared pan. Bake until golden and firm throughout, 30–40 minutes. Entire top should be light brown, and the mixture should be firm when shaken slightly. While cake is baking, make cream topping.

Cream Topping

In mixer bowl, whip cream on high for 2–3 minutes, until soft peaks are formed. Add evaporated milk, condensed milk, and liqueur. Beat on medium speed for 2 minutes.

Remove cake from oven. Use a toothpick or skewer to make deep holes in the top, about every inch or so. While cake is still warm, slowly pour cream topping over cake. Cool to room temperature; cover and refrigerate until well chilled, at least 4 hours. Note that middle of cake may sink; you can even out surface using frosting.

Frosting

Beat ingredients with an electric mixer on high speed until stiff peaks form. Frost chilled cake. Serve with toppings as desired.

Veggies and Sides

Sweet Pea Puree

Serves 4

Peas are a good source of fiber, vitamins A, B6, and C, magnesium, and iron.

Serving Ideas

Goes well with salmon, other fish dishes, chicken, and turkey.

Ingredients

12 oz. frozen peas, cooked in microwave according to package directions, and cooled slightly

¼ cup fresh mint leaves, or 2 tsp. dried mint

3 cloves peeled garlic

½ tsp. kosher salt

½ tsp. freshly ground black pepper

2 tbsp. extra virgin olive oil

½ cup finely grated Parmesan cheese, plus extra for garnish

1 tbsp. cider vinegar

Optional: extra Parmesan, for garnish

Directions

Combine all ingredients in a food processor. Pulse until combined. If mixture is too thick, add water.

Marinated Grilled Vegetables

Makes 1 cup marinade—enough for about 8 cups of raw veggies

Serving Ideas

For a sandwich or a wrap, spread chimichurri or pesto on bread or wrap, and add goat or Feta cheese, and/or mashed avocado. Fill with grilled veggies. From the fridge or pantry, add roasted red bell peppers or sun-dried tomatoes to grilled veggies.

Balsamic Marinade

⅔ cup olive oil

⅓ cup balsamic vinegar

1 heaping tsp. dried thyme, rosemary, or your favorite herb

5 cloves minced garlic

½ tsp. dry mustard or 1 tsp. prepared Dijon mustard, to bind oil and vinegar

1 tsp. kosher salt

½ tsp. black pepper

Asian-Inspired Marinade

This works well for asparagus and eggplant: 2 tbsp. white miso, 1 tbsp. soy sauce, 1 tbsp. grated ginger, ¼ cup vegetable or peanut oil, and 2 tbsp. seasoned rice wine vinegar.

Chimichurri Marinade

See separate recipe for chimichurri sauce. If using chimichurri, use a slightly lower grilling temperature, and add 1–2 tbsp. olive oil to sauce recipe, to prevent drying out.

Directions

Combine all marinade ingredients in a small bowl; mix well. Place cut-up veggies in a large Ziploc bag. Pour marinade over; allow to sit for at least 30 minutes and up to 2 hours, turning at least once. Approximate grill times below are for medium heat, stovetop grill.

- **Portobello mushrooms**: 5 minutes (3 on first side, 2 on second side)
- **Asparagus spears**, medium thickness: 10 minutes (6 minutes first side, 4 minutes second side)
- **Zucchini**, about ¼-inch thick: 5 minutes (3 and 2)

- **Onion,** sliced sweet: about 5 minutes (3 and 2)
- **Peppers** (e.g., jalapeno, red bell, halved): 7 minutes (4 and 3)
- **Roma tomatoes**, halved: 5 minutes (3 on first side, 2 on second side)
- **Eggplant** Slice thinly (¼–½ inch). Cook on slightly lower heat for 6–7 minutes (4 and 3). For an unusual appetizer, use slender eggplant. Place few crumbles of goat cheese on cooked eggplant slice. Add several julienned strips of sun-dried tomato from a jar, including a bit of oil. Roll up and secure with a toothpick. Sprinkle with Parmesan cheese.

Reconstructed Turnips

4–6 servings

You can make just the turnip bottoms if you like (go to step 3). For the greens, you can substitute mustard greens. Some groceries have limited availability, depending on the season. Turnips are a very good source of vitamins A, C, K, folate, calcium, and fiber.

Greens

2–3 pieces bacon, or 2 oz. ham, chopped
1–2 tbsp. bacon grease or olive oil
2 medium turnips, including greens, divided
   (greens rinsed, tough ribs removed)

Optional: 2–3 carrots, or ½ of a sweet potato
½ cup water, chicken broth, or vegetable broth for
   cooking turnip greens
Optional: hot sauce to taste

Turnip Puree

1 tsp. kosher salt

¼ cup fresh orange juice

¼ cup maple syrup

2 tbsp. butter—regular or light

2 tsp. grated ginger or ½ tsp. powdered ginger

Salt and pepper to taste

Directions

To make the greens, cook bacon over medium heat in a Dutch oven until crispy. Remove bacon and chop. Leave 1–2 tbsp. bacon grease in the pan. Alternatively, heat 2 tbsp. olive oil over medium heat. Fry ham pieces for 2 minutes; leave in pan.

Chop greens coarsely and add to hot pan along with water or broth. Reduce heat to medium-low, cover loosely, and cook, stirring several times, until tender and most liquid has evaporated, 10–12 minutes. Add bacon bits again, stir, and remove from heat. Add hot sauce if desired.

To make turnip puree, peel turnip bottoms and cut turnip, carrots, or peeled sweet potato into ½-inch chunks. Place in a saucepan, barely cover with water, and add salt. Bring to a boil over medium-high heat.

Lower heat to medium, cover loosely, and cook at a low boil for 10 minutes. Uncover and cook until tender and most water has evaporated, stirring occasionally, 10–15 minutes more. Add orange juice, maple syrup, and butter. Stir to combine and to melt butter.

Use a hand blender or food processor to puree turnip mixture to desired consistency. Add ginger, salt, and pepper. If mixture is watery, return to saucepan and heat over medium-low heat to thicken.

Serve turnip puree mounded over greens.

Creamed Spinach

4 servings

Try incorporating in Eggs Sardou (separate recipe) or see soufflé and dip options below.

A classic, served alongside steak with béarnaise. This is a lighter and tangier version than some.

Health benefits of spinach include potassium, vitamins C and K, and heart-healthy folate.

Ingredients

4 tbsp. butter—regular or light

10 oz. baby spinach

2 oz. grated Parmesan cheese (or try crumbled Feta or cotija)

¼ cup plain Greek yogurt

½ tsp. dried mustard or 1 tsp. Dijon mustard

¼ tsp. freshly grated nutmeg

Kosher salt and freshly ground black pepper, to taste

Directions

Melt butter in a Dutch oven over medium heat. Working in 4 batches, add spinach to pot, tossing with tongs to wilt. This only takes a couple minutes. Stir in cheese, yogurt, mustard, and nutmeg. When cheese is melted, remove from heat. Using an immersion blender, purée spinach mixture until smooth. Season to taste with salt and pepper.

Individual Soufflés

Prepare as directed above. Separate 2 eggs. Stir egg yolks into slightly cooled spinach mixture. In a small, deep bowl, beat 2 egg whites until stiff peaks form. Beat in 1 tsp. white vinegar. Gradually fold egg whites into spinach-egg yolk mixture. Pour into individual ramekins.

Preheat oven to 350 degrees. Bake for 20–25 minutes. Soufflé is done when the center springs back when touched lightly and edges are just beginning to brown.

Spinach-Artichoke Dip

Add about ½ can of artichokes, drained, rinsed, and chopped, to basic recipe. If desired, add 2–3 oz. of your favorite white cheese for a richer flavor. Stir in 1–2 tsp. hot sauce if desired.

For saag paneer (spinach with Indian flavors)

In general, follow directions for creamed spinach: see below for exact instructions. In ingredients list, eliminate mustard and nutmeg. Substitute 4 oz. cubed non-melting white cheese such as paneer, feta or cotija for the parmesan . In a small bowl, toss cubes with a mixture of: ½ tsp. turmeric, dash cayenne pepper, 1 tsp. onion powder, 1 tsp. garlic powder, ½ tsp. cumin, ½ tsp. coriander, and 1 tbsp. grated ginger. Set aside. Follow directions for creamed spinach, through wilting spinach. Add yogurt. Puree spinach and yogurt using immersion blender. Reduce heat to low; add cheese cube mixture. Cook 8-10 minutes, to blend flavors.

Lemon Butter Broccoli, Green Beans, or Asparagus

4–6 servings

Vegetables

1 bunch broccoli, tough stems removed, 1 lb. green beans, trimmed, or 1 lb. asparagus spears, tough stems removed

1 recipe lemon-butter sauce— see separate recipe in Sauces

Optional: toasted slivered almonds

Garlic salt (or onion salt) and pepper, to taste

Directions

Steam broccoli, green beans, or asparagus 3–6 minutes, until crisp-tender. Drizzle with lemon butter sauce; top with almonds if desired.

Asparagus or Green Bean Gratin

6–8 servings

Asparagus is a top antioxidant food, with high amounts of vitamins A and C, iron, and folate. Green beans, also high in antioxidants, are good sources of vitamins A, C, and K, and fiber. Citrus zests are high in fiber and flavonoids, which fight cancer and diabetes and lower cholesterol.

Ingredients

1½–2 lb. asparagus or green beans, trimmed
1 cup prepared Bechamel sauce (separate recipe)
Optional: 3 oz. goat cheese
Zest and juice of 1 lemon: about 2 tbsp. juice and
   2 tsp. zest

¼ cup pine nuts, slivered almonds or chopped
   walnuts
½ cup finely grated Parmesan cheese

Directions

Coat baking dish with nonstick spray. Preheat oven to 375 degrees.

In a saucepan, steam asparagus until it starts to become tender, about 2–3 minutes; green beans may take 4–5 minutes. Place in prepared baking dish.

Meanwhile, combine Bechamel, goat cheese, lemon juice, and lemon zest. Pour cheese mixture over asparagus or beans; toss lightly to combine. Top with nuts and Parmesan cheese. Cook until dish is bubbling, 15–20 minutes.

Roasted Cauliflower with Browned Butter

6 servings

Cauliflower contains antioxidants and has cancer-fighting properties. Its vitamin K fights inflammation.

Ingredients

1 large head cauliflower, rinsed and cut into 1-inch pieces	4 tbsp. butter
	Garlic salt and black pepper to taste

Directions

Preheat oven to 400 degrees. Heat butter in a small saucepan over medium-low heat for several minutes, until butter begins to brown.

   Meanwhile place cauliflower florets on a foil- or parchment-lined baking sheet. Drizzle with browned butter. Roast until beginning to brown, about 20 minutes, checking after 15 minutes. Sprinkle with garlic salt and pepper.

Cauliflower Puree with Truffle Oil

Makes about 4 cups puree

Think of this as a low-carb substitute for grits. Try it as a base for wild mushroom sauce and for shrimp; see separate recipe for shrimp and grits.

Underrated cauliflower is a good source of vitamins B6, C, and K. It fights heart disease and cancer.

Ingredients

1 medium to large head cauliflower, core removed, cut into florets

1–2 tbsp. olive oil, from a spray can (enough to coat the cauliflower)

Dash salt

1 cup milk, preferably whole milk; or ½ cup evaporated milk and ½ cup water

1 cup chicken or vegetable broth

3 oz. cream cheese

1 tsp. garlic powder

1 tbsp. butter— regular or light

Optional: 1–2 tbsp. truffle oil (very yummy!) or 3–4 oz. grated Parmesan or white cheddar cheese

Salt and pepper to taste

Directions

Preheat oven to 400 degrees. Place cauliflower florets on parchment- or foil-lined baking sheet. Drizzle or spray cauliflower with 1–2 tbsp. olive oil. Sprinkle with salt. Let sit 10 minutes while you preheat oven. Roast 15–20 minutes, until tender and just starting to brown.

Place in a Dutch oven; add milk, broth, cream cheese, garlic powder, and butter. Bring to a boil over medium heat; reduce to low and simmer 10 minutes, stirring occasionally. Blend to desired consistency with an immersion blender.

Add truffle oil or Parmesan cheese if desired. Simmer another 10 minutes, stirring often. Note that mixture will thicken somewhat upon standing.

Creamy Kohlrabi Puree with Fennel

Makes about 3 cups puree

Kohlrabi is a German word meaning "cabbage turnip."

It's a member of the brassica family, along with kale, Brussels sprouts, broccoli, and cauliflower, and its phytochemicals are highly regarded for their antioxidant properties. Kohlrabi is a good source of potassium and fiber, vitamin B6, and vitamin C.

This recipe can be used in butternut squash and kale lasagna (separate recipe) or served as a side dish.

Ingredients

2–3 kohlrabi bulbs, peeled and cut into ½-inch chunks

1 large fennel bulb, thinly sliced, fronds saved

1 tsp. kosher salt

⅓ cup heavy cream, evaporated milk, or half and half

4 tbsp. butter—regular or light

Dash of freshly grated nutmeg

Salt and white or black pepper to taste

Directions

Place kohlrabi and fennel bulb in a heavy saucepan; barely cover with water and add salt. Cover and heat to a boil over medium-high heat. Reduce heat to medium. Cover loosely and cook 10 minutes. Uncover and cook about 20–30 minutes, until very tender and much of the water has evaporated. Remaining liquid will be syrupy.

   Add butter, cream, and nutmeg; stir gently. Puree with a handheld immersion blender. Garnish with fronds.

Rutabaga and Carrot Puree

4–6 servings

Rutabagas are a good source of vitamins B6 and C, fiber, potassium, and calcium. They are a cross between a cabbage and a turnip.

The name comes from the old Swedish word *Rotabagge*, meaning "ram root." It was discussed as early as 1620 by a Swedish botanist. In the United States, the plant is also known as Swedish turnip or yellow turnip.

In this recipe, adjust the proportions of carrots and rutabagas to your liking or try a 2:1 ratio of rutabaga to carrot, by weight.

Ingredients

2 medium rutabagas, peeled and diced into
 ½-inch pieces
2–3 carrots, peeled and cut into ½-inch pieces
1 tsp. salt—more to taste

3 tbsp. butter—regular or light
2 tbsp. sour cream or plain Greek yogurt
Pepper to taste
Optional: 1–2 tbsp. honey or maple syrup

Directions

Place rutabaga and carrot pieces in a saucepan. Barely cover with water; add salt. Bring to a boil over high heat; reduce heat to medium. Cook, uncovered, stirring often during the last 5 minutes, until vegetables are soft and water has been reduced substantially, about 20 minutes total.

Drain if necessary, being mindful that there are nutrients in the cooking water.

Add remaining ingredients; toss to coat. If you prefer a smooth consistency, blend with a hand immersion blender to make a puree. Adjust seasonings.

Cheesy Pan-Fried Eggplant Patties

Makes 12–16 patties, serving 6–8

Eggplant contains cholesterol-lowering pectin, and it may help keep skin looking young. Some studies show an ability to fight the onset of Alzheimer's disease.

Eggplant was cultivated in China and India as early as the fifth century. It was introduced into Spain by Arabs in the twelfth century, but it was slow to catch on.

If you know someone who relates to the Spanish who wouldn't eat it, give this recipe a try. Cheese and crackers make everything taste better!

Ingredients

1 medium eggplant (about 1½ lb.)

3–4 tbsp. olive oil, divided

1 "sleeve" Ritz crackers—about 30 crackers, crushed and divided

1¼ cups grated sharp cheddar cheese

1 large egg, lightly beaten

3 tbsp. minced fresh parsley, preferably flat-leaf

3 tbsp. chopped green onion

3 garlic cloves, minced

½ tsp. kosher salt

¼ tsp. black pepper

Directions

Cut eggplant in half lengthwise. Spray flesh with olive oil. Bake, flesh sides down, on a parchment- or foil-lined baking sheet at 400 degrees for 35–40 minutes, until very tender. Cool; scoop flesh into a medium size bowl. Drain off excess liquid. Mash well with a potato masher (or use a knife and fork).

Mix cooled eggplant, 1 cup cracker crumbs, cheese, egg, parsley, onion, garlic, salt, and pepper. Shape into patties. Refrigerate at least 30 minutes to combine flavors and prevent crumbling during cooking.

Place remaining cracker crumbs on a rimmed plate. Coat eggplant patties lightly on both sides.

Heat 2 tbsp. oil in a large nonstick skillet over medium heat. Add patties, several at a time; don't crowd the pan. Shake the pan a bit to keep patties from sticking. Carefully turn after about 3 minutes. When bottoms are deep golden, flip and cook another 3 minutes.

Fried Eggplant, Zucchini, or Artichokes with Beer Batter Crust

Serving Ideas

Try with creamy cucumber dressing. See veggie variations below.

Ingredients

1¾ cups all-purpose flour

1 tsp. baking powder

1 tsp. black pepper (or ½ tsp. cayenne pepper)

1 tsp. salt or Creole seasoning (such as Tony Chachere's)

12 oz. beer

1 large eggplant, sliced thinly, to about ¼-inch thick (no need to peel)

Vegetable or olive oil for frying (¼-inch depth in frying pan)

Directions

Whisk together dry ingredients. Stir in beer to make batter. It's okay to have some small lumps.

Place oil in frying pan. Heat over medium heat for about 3 minutes. Test oil temperature: see if a drop of water spatters in it. Dip eggplant into batter, then place in hot oil. Cover the pan with a loose-fitting lid or one with a steam vent, to minimize splattering. Be careful when you turn the slices.

Cook 4 minutes on first side, checking after 3 minutes, until lightly browned, then turn and cook another 3 minutes. Drain on paper towels.

Subsequent batches may cook more quickly since pan may be hotter than the first round. Serve piping hot. If necessary, reheat at 300 degrees for 10–15 minutes.

Appetizer Option

Make recipe above using Japanese eggplant or another long, slender version. Slice crosswise to make discs. Top with goat cheese, then red bell pepper pesto, sun-dried tomato pesto, or summer tomato jam (separate recipes).

Variation

Try other veggies, such as sliced zucchini, Portobello mushrooms, or quartered artichoke hearts.

Onion Rings

Use enough batter so the rings are somewhat linked together in the frying pan. This will make turning them easier.

Pan-Fried Fish

You can use the same beer batter for fish, such as cod. Just heat ⅛-inch olive oil in a frying pan over medium heat. Cook coated fish 6–8 minutes, turning once.

White Bean Gratin

Serves 6–8 as a side dish, 10–12 as an appetizer dip

White beans—including navy beans and cannellini—contain many minerals, including calcium, iron, magnesium, and potassium. They are heart-healthy and a good source of fiber.

Serving Ideas

This can be served as a vegetable or dip.

Ingredients

½ cup grated Gruyere or Swiss cheese

½ cup grated Fontina cheese

¼ cup grated Parmesan cheese

½ cup panko breadcrumbs

3 tbsp. olive oil, divided

1 large shallot, minced

1 tsp. dried rosemary, crushed to release flavor

1 tsp. dried thyme

4 garlic cloves, minced

1 cup low-sodium chicken or vegetable broth

3 tbsp. plain Greek yogurt

Salt and pepper to taste

2 14-oz. cans cannellini beans, drained and rinsed

Directions

Preheat oven to 375 degrees. Meanwhile, in a medium bowl, combine cheeses with panko breadcrumbs; set aside.

In a large skillet, heat 2 tbsp. olive oil over medium heat. Add shallot, rosemary, and thyme. Cook until soft, about 5 minutes. Add minced garlic; cook 30 seconds. Add broth, yogurt, salt, and pepper to the skillet; stir to combine. Add beans and stir gently, in order not to break up the beans.

Simmer 15 minutes, stirring occasionally, until liquid is somewhat reduced and mixture is fragrant. Note that liquid will be further reduced during baking.

Coat a baking dish with nonstick spray. Scoop bean mixture into dish. Sprinkle cheese and breadcrumb mixture over top. Drizzle with remaining olive oil. Bake for about 25 minutes, until top is golden and bubbly.

Mashed Maple Sweet Potatoes

About 6 servings

Sweet potatoes contain vitamins A, B6, C, and E, and several minerals; they have more beta-carotene than any other veggie, and they provide cancer-fighting benefits.

Ingredients

2 lb. sweet potatoes (2–3 potatoes, depending on size)

¼ cup plain Greek yogurt

4 tbsp. butter—regular or light

3 tbsp. maple syrup; more to taste

¼ cup orange juice

Salt and pepper to taste

Directions

Preheat oven to 400 degrees. Rinse potatoes. Prick; rub with olive oil. Pack tightly in foil. Bake directly on oven rack until very tender, 45–60 min. Cool slightly, then peel. Mash with remaining ingredients.

Twice-Baked Loaded Mashed Potato Casserole

8–12 servings

For entertaining, I like making muffin-size potatoes, which are a little fancier than a casserole. See directions at end of recipe. For easy baked bacon, place raw bacon slices on a nonstick, foil-lined baking pan. Bake at 375 degrees 10–14 minutes. Chop into bits.

Potatoes are a good source of vitamins B6 and C, potassium, fiber, and iron.

Ingredients

2–3 Russet potatoes, about 1½ lb. total

4 tbsp. butter—regular or light—cut into several pieces

1 cup ricotta cheese

½ cup plain Greek yogurt (reduce to ¼ cup if using Velveeta)

1 tsp. dried oregano, marjoram, or rosemary

1 tsp. dried mustard or 2 tsp. Dijon mustard

½ cup buttermilk

½ cup loosely packed bacon bits, to taste

⅓ cup chopped green onions or shallots—plus 3 tbsp. more for topping

1 tsp. hot sauce (such as Frank's), more to taste

Garlic salt and black pepper to taste

8 oz. grated cheddar cheese or Velveeta

Directions

Prick potatoes in several places with a fork. Rinse and wrap in a paper towel. Microwave on high until tender, about 7–9 minutes, or use programmed setting. Cool slightly; peel.

Mash potato filling with ingredients through pepper. Stir 6 oz. of cheddar cheese into potato mixture (if using Velveeta, use all 8 oz.). Top with remaining grated cheddar and extra chopped green onion.

Place in a greased baking dish. Cover with foil; bake at 350 degrees for 20 minutes. Remove foil; bake until mixture is hot and cheese has melted, 10–15 minutes longer.

For muffin-sized potatoes, line a muffin tin with paper liners (using parchment if available). Coat lightly with nonstick spray (no need to spray if using parchment); bake at 350 for 20-30 minutes.

Butternut Squash Soufflé

8–12 servings

Great festive dish for Thanksgiving or Christmas! Thanks to my friend Jennifer for sharing her family recipe, to which I made modest changes. For a change, try another type of winter squash or pumpkin. You can also top with sweet and spicy pecans (separate recipe) instead of regular toasted pecans.

Ingredients

2 lb. butternut squash (makes about 2 cups mashed squash)

3 tbsp. craisins or dried cherries

¼ cup orange juice

2 tbsp. cornstarch

1 tsp. kosher salt

¼ cup maple syrup or lightly packed brown sugar

3 large eggs, separated

½ cup (1 stick) butter—regular or light—melted and cooled

½ cup heavy whipping cream

1 tsp. white vinegar (for beating egg whites)

½ cup toasted pecans or walnuts

Directions

Preheat oven to 375. Halve the squash; remove seeds. Place, cut sides down, in a baking pan with about 1 inch of water. Bake until tender when pierced, 50–60 minutes. Remove from oven and cool.

Mash squash well. Reduce oven temperature to 350.

Meanwhile, soak dried fruit in orange juice for at least 10 minutes. Drain fruit, saving juice. Dissolve cornstarch in juice. Combine with an electric mixer: mashed squash, salt, maple syrup, corn starch/juice mixture, egg yolks, and butter. Mix well; stir in cream.

In a separate bowl, beat egg whites until sudsy. Add vinegar and continue to beat to glossy peaks. Fold egg whites into squash mixture, gently but thoroughly. Pour into 2-quart baking dish.

Bake casserole at 350 for 45 minutes. Sprinkle with nuts and fruit; bake another 5–10 minutes, until very firm. Note: deep casseroles may take an hour or longer.

Spaghetti Squash with Mediterranean Flavors

4–6 servings

Spaghetti squash is a handy, low-carb, low-calorie substitute for pasta. One cup, prepared, has fewer than fifty calories and provides a good amount of fiber and vitamin C.

Ingredients

1 spaghetti squash, halved lengthwise and seeded
2 tbsp. olive oil
1 small red onion or a large shallot, minced
2 cloves garlic, minced
1 cup chopped ripe tomatoes
4 oz. crumbled Feta cheese

½ cup chopped peppers such as red or green bell pepper, or poblano pepper
Optional: 1–2 tbsp. capers or chopped Kalamata olives (with 1–2 tbsp. brine if desired)
2 tbsp. chopped fresh basil or parsley
Garlic salt and black pepper to taste
Optional: 1–2 tbsp. lemon juice, for drizzling

Directions

Preheat oven to 375. Pour water into a 13x9x2 baking dish to a depth of about an inch. Place squash halves, cut sides down, in prepared pan. Bake 45–60 minutes, until a sharp knife can be inserted with only a little resistance. Meanwhile, combine remaining ingredients in a small bowl.

Remove squash from oven. Set aside to cool enough to be easily handled. Use a large fork to scoop the flesh from the squash and place in a medium bowl. Toss with tomato mixture.

Adjust flavorings. Drizzle with lemon juice if desired. Serve warm, reheating in a microwave if necessary.

Additional Ideas

Bake as above, then:

- Serve with garlic salt as a base for Italian meatballs and marinara. Or toss with chopped bacon and a bit of bacon grease.
- Use as you would sauerkraut in a Reuben sandwich, by tossing with lemon juice and caraway seeds.
- Make spaghetti squash "al Limone", topped with lemon butter sauce (separate recipe).
- Toss cooked squash with red or green pesto (store-bought or separate recipes).

Yellow Squash Casserole

6–8 servings

Yellow squash is a good source of potassium, vitamin B6, and vitamin C; its high fiber content helps regulate blood sugar.

Ingredients

2 lb. yellow squash (4–5 large squash)

1–2 tbsp. olive oil (just enough to coat squash slices lightly)

1 tsp. kosher salt

1 cup chopped onion

2 tsp. dried marjoram or oregano

3 tbsp. butter—regular or light

18 buttery round crackers such as Ritz, crushed

4 oz. (1 cup) grated cheddar cheese; or use American cheese such as Velveeta

2 large eggs, beaten
Salt and pepper to taste

Optional: up to 1 cup frozen peas

Directions

Preheat oven to 400 degrees. Remove peas from freezer; set aside at room temperature.

Slice squash crosswise, thinly. In a medium bowl, toss squash with just enough olive oil to coat. Sprinkle with salt; stir well. Pour out squash onto a parchment or foil lined cookie sheet. Roast until very tender, 20-25 minutes. Remove from oven. Lower oven temperature to 350 degrees.

In medium bowl, mix roasted squash with ingredients through pepper; stir well. Place in a greased casserole dish. Bake in preheated 350 degree oven for 25-30 minutes, or until bubbly. Stir peas into piping-hot casserole as soon as you remove from oven.

Corn Cakes

Makes about eight 4-inch wide corn cakes or about a dozen silver-dollar sized appetizers

Corn is a good source of vitamin C, protein, and fiber. Recent studies show a link between fiber and decreased heart disease risk. Yellow corn has eyesight benefits.

Serving Ideas

Use as a base for shrimp and grits, with corn cakes subbing for grits, with goat cheese and hot pepper jelly, with red bell pepper pesto, as a base for Eggs Benedict or Eggs Sardou.

Have a sweet tooth? Try spreading a little butter over a hot corn cake, then drizzle with maple syrup.

Ingredients

2 cups corn kernels from fresh corn (or use canned corn, drained, or frozen corn, thawed)

1 large egg, lightly beaten

¼ cup buttermilk

2 tbsp. butter, melted

¼ cup flour

¼ cup yellow cornmeal

Optional: ⅓ cup grated or crumbled white cheese of your choice

2 tbsp. minced shallot or green onion

Optional: 2 tbsp. minced bell pepper or poblano pepper

½ tsp. salt

½ tsp. pepper or smoked paprika

2–3 tbsp. olive oil

Preparation

Pulse corn in a food processor 3 to 4 times, just until corn is coarsely chopped. Stir together ingredients through black pepper in a large bowl, just until dry ingredients are moistened. Add corn.

Heat a nonstick skillet and 1 tbsp. oil over medium heat. Spoon batter for each cake onto hot skillet; do not spread or flatten cakes. Cook 3 to 4 minutes, until tops are covered with bubbles and edges look cooked, checking after 2 minutes to make sure they aren't burning. Turn and cook other side for 2 to 3 minutes, adding more oil to pan as necessary.

Couscous Cakes

4–6 servings

This is a handy use for leftover couscous. Serve as a base or accompaniment for soup or stew. Or serve with a pepper jelly, such as apricot-pepper, and a dollop of plain yogurt or sour cream.

Citrus zests are high in fiber and flavonoids, which fight cancer and diabetes, and lower cholesterol.

Ingredients

2 cups cooked couscous, prepared according to package instructions, cooled

¼ cup chopped fresh cilantro or parsley leaves (or 2 tsp. coriander/cilantro chutney)

2 eggs

1½ tsp. ground coriander

Juice and zest of 1 lemon (about 2 tbsp. juice and 2 tsp. zest)

1 tsp. kosher salt

½ tsp. freshly ground black pepper or smoked paprika

2 tbsp. all-purpose flour

¼ cup olive oil

Directions

In a medium bowl, combine couscous, cilantro, eggs, coriander, lemon juice, zest, salt, and pepper. Sprinkle flour over the mixture. Mix until combined. Form 8 patties.

In a large nonstick skillet, heat 1 tbsp. oil over medium heat. Add half the patties and cook for 3½–4 minutes, until golden. Turn cakes over, add 1 more tbsp. oil, and cook 2½–3 minutes.

Drain on paper towels. Repeat.

Gorgonzola Grits

8–10 servings

If you're not a fan of Gorgonzola cheese, try a combination of Parmesan and goat cheeses.

Ingredients

2 cups low-sodium chicken broth (or shrimp broth, if making shrimp and grits)

1 can (12 oz.) evaporated milk

4 oz. cream cheese

¼ cup plain Greek yogurt

1 cup quick-cooking grits (the 5–minute kind, not instant)

6 oz. Gorgonzola cheese

Salt and pepper to taste

Directions

Heat broth, milk, cream cheese, and yogurt over medium heat until cheese is melted and mixture is beginning to boil. Whisk in grits. Stir; lower heat to medium low. Cover; cook about 5 minutes, stirring occasionally, until grits are cooked and mixture is thick. Stir in Gorgonzola until it's melted. Remove from heat; add salt and pepper to taste.

Toasted Almond Rice

8 servings

This is very easy, yet it is fancy enough for guests. For a change, try pine nuts instead of almonds.

Ingredients

3 oz. (1 cup) sliced almonds

2 tbs. unsalted butter—regular or light

2 tbsp. olive oil

2 large shallots, minced (or ½ of a red onion, minced)

2 cups basmati rice, rinsed and drained

2 cups chicken broth or vegetable broth, preferably low-sodium

Zest and juice of 1 lemon (about 2 tbsp. juice and 2 tsp. zest)

2 cups water

1 tsp. kosher salt

½ tsp. black pepper

Directions

Preheat oven to 325 degrees. Toast almonds until golden brown, 5–7 minutes. Remove from oven. Increase oven temperature to 350.

In a Dutch oven or large ovenproof saucepan with lid, heat butter and oil over medium heat. Add shallots and cook, stirring, until softened, 3 to 5 minutes. Add rice; stir until all grains are well coated. Add chicken broth, water, lemon juice/zest, salt, and pepper; bring to a boil.

Cover pot, transfer to oven, and bake until rice is tender and liquid is absorbed, 20 to 25 minutes. Remove from oven. Let stand, covered, 5 minutes. Fluff with a fork, stir in toasted almonds, and serve.

Golden Turmeric Rice

4 servings

This has a pretty golden color and goes well with south Asian food. In terms of flavor, it's similar to saffron rice, and it is much less expensive to make.

Turmeric is a member of the ginger family. It has anti-inflammatory, antiviral, and antibacterial properties, and it is believed to be beneficial in fighting cancer, diabetes, and Alzheimer's disease.

Serving Idea

For a main-dish vegetarian meal, my friend Amy substitutes fresh grated ginger for the thyme. Instead of chicken broth, use half veggie broth and half light coconut milk. Stir in cooked lentils for a complete vegetarian entree. Brown rice would work just as nicely.

Ingredients

2 tbsp. butter—regular or light
¼ cup minced sweet onion or shallot
2 minced garlic cloves
1 cup raw basmati or jasmine rice
2 tsp. turmeric
2 cups chicken broth or vegetable broth,
    preferably low-sodium

1 bay leaf
½ tsp. thyme
Salt and pepper to taste
Optional: chopped cilantro or parsley (for
    garnish) and 1 tbsp. olive oil (for drizzling on
    cooked rice)

Directions

Melt butter in saucepan over medium heat. Add onion and garlic; cook until softened, about 3 minutes. Add rice and turmeric; stir to coat. Add remaining ingredients; bring to a boil.

Cover; reduce heat to on medium-low and simmer 16–18 minutes, until tender. Remove bay leaf. Taste for seasonings.

Desserts

Carrot Cake

Serves 10–12

I lightened this recipe in calories and density by replacing some of the oil with orange juice. In addition, I also added orange zest, which has concentrated nutrients. For a different frosting, try orange cream (separate recipe).

Ingredients

2 cups all-purpose flour

1½ cups granulated sugar

½ tsp. salt

1 tsp. baking soda

1 tsp. ground cinnamon

½ tsp. freshly ground nutmeg

½ tsp. ground cardamom

3 large eggs

1 cup vegetable oil

½ cup freshly squeezed orange juice (1 tbsp. zest reserved)

2 tsp. vanilla extract

1 tbsp. orange zest

3–4 carrots, to yield 2 cups grated carrots

1–8 oz. can crushed pineapple, well drained

1 cup flaked coconut

1¼ cups chopped walnuts or pecans, toasted and divided

Directions

Preheat oven to 350 degrees. In a large mixing bowl, whisk together dry ingredients through cardamom. Add eggs, oil, orange juice, and vanilla; beat 3 minutes on medium speed.

Stir in zest, grated carrots, pineapple, coconut, and ¾ cup walnuts. Pour into a greased and floured 13x9x2–inch baking pan, two 8- to 9-inch cake pans, or about 24 cupcake liners. Bake at 350 for 50 to 60 minutes (35–40 minutes for two pans and 20–25 minutes for cupcakes), or until top is brown and springs back to the touch.

Cool on a rack. Frost cooled cake with cream cheese frosting and sprinkle with remaining chopped nuts, pressing into the frosting very lightly.

Cream Cheese Frosting

8 oz. cream cheese, softened

12 tbsp. (1½ sticks) unsalted butter, softened

1 tsp. vanilla extract

3 cups powdered sugar

Dash salt

Mix cream cheese, butter, and vanilla in bowl with an electric mixer. Beat on medium speed until combined. Add sugar and salt; mix until smooth. Spread over cooled cake. Sprinkle with nuts.

Lemon Pudding Bundt Cake

10–12 servings

This nostalgic recipe was one of my favorites to make growing up. Recently I found it, handwritten, in a stained spiral notebook from eighth grade.

Cake

½ cup butter (1 stick), room temperature
¾ cup sugar
2 tsp. vanilla extract
3 large eggs
2½ cups flour

1 tsp. baking soda
1 tsp. kosher salt
1 3.4-oz. container instant lemon pudding mix
1 cup buttermilk
12 oz. mango or apricot nectar

Lemon Glaze

2 cups powdered sugar
5 tbsp. butter, melted

4 tbsp. fresh lemon juice (from about 2 lemons)
1 tbsp. lemon zest

Directions

Preheat oven to 325 degrees; grease and flour a Bundt or tube pan. Place pan on cookie sheet in case it overflows a bit in the oven. Mix softened butter and sugar until fluffy. Add vanilla and eggs, beating 2 minutes on medium speed.

Whisk together dry ingredients. Add to egg mixture, alternating with nectar and buttermilk. Pour batter into Bundt pan. Bake for 45–50 minutes, using a toothpick to make certain cake is done. Cool completely on a rack.

While cake is baking, prepare glaze by combining all ingredients in a small bowl. Set aside.

Invert cooled cake onto a platter; poke it all over with a bamboo or metal skewer, or long-tined fork. Drizzle with glaze.

Ricotta Cake

8 servings

This is like an airy cheesecake without a crust. Its subtle, fruity flavor is great for a light, refreshing dessert.

Topping Ideas

Try whipped cream and orange-macerated peaches (see below), curacao sauce, or blueberry sauce—or use your favorite fruit preserves, heated to drizzling consistency. For pumpkin chiffon cake, see directions below.

Citrus zests are high in fiber and flavonoids, which fight cancer and diabetes, and lower cholesterol.

Originally from Italy's Lombardy region, mascarpone likely originated southwest of Milan in the late sixteenth or early seventeenth century. According to culinary experts, the cheese's original name was "mascherpone," derived from "Cascina Mascherpa," a family farmhouse that was located between Milan and Pavia.

Ingredients

⅔ cup granulated sugar

6 large eggs, divided (plus 1 tsp. white vinegar for beating egg whites)

8 oz. whole-milk ricotta

8 oz. tub mascarpone cheese

3 tbsp. flour

1 tsp. baking powder

1 tbsp. orange zest

2 tbsp. orange juice

2 tbsp. Curacao or Grand Marnier (or additional orange juice)

½ tsp. kosher salt

Directions

If making orange-macerated peaches, do that first since flavor improves with time.

Preheat oven to 350 degrees. Place a pan of hot water on lower shelf of oven as you preheat. Add cake ingredients, including the 6 egg yolks but not the whites, to a food processor in the order listed, pulsing briefly after each addition. After all ingredients have been added, process 2–3 minutes, until smooth. Transfer to mixing bowl and set aside.

In a small, deep mixer bowl, use an electric hand mixer to beat the 6 egg whites until just short of stiff peaks. Beat in vinegar. Gently fold egg whites into ricotta mixture.

Pour batter into a generously sprayed or buttered 9-inch springform pan. Line the outside with foil, going up 1 inch of the sides to prevent drips. Place pan on a thin (non-insulated) baking sheet. Bake until center of cake springs back when touched, about 45 minutes. Immediately release sides of pan to minimize cracking on surface.

Serve cake at room temperature, topped with whipped cream and berries or the topping of your choice.

Note: if the top cracks, simply use topping to cover.

Orange Macerated Peach Topping

4–5 ripe peaches or mangoes, peeled and sliced

1 cup freshly squeezed orange juice

3 tbsp. orange-flavored liqueur, such as Triple Sec, Grand Marnier, or Curacao (or 1 tbsp. honey)

Directions

Combine all ingredients in a bowl. Stir well; let sit at least 30 minutes.

Variation: Pumpkin Chiffon Cake

Follow directions for ricotta cake, adding 8 oz. canned pumpkin puree. Top with Curacao sauce (separate recipe) or whipped cream, if desired.

French Silk Pie

6–8 servings

French silk pie was one of the tastiest dishes my mother made when I was growing up in the 1960's and 70's. Funny that an Internet search says it was invented in 1987! I'm inclined to believe several sources who say it was invented by the winner of Pillsbury's third annual bake-off in 1951: Betty Cooper, from

Kensington, Maryland. Thank you, Betty! This recipe has more chocolate but the same spirit. Note: filling freezes well.

Ingredients

1 cup heavy cream (plus an optional second cup for topping)

Optional: ¼ cup powdered sugar for each 1 cup cream (to keep whipped cream stiff)

3 large eggs

¾ cup sugar

½ tsp. salt

2 tbsp. water

8 oz. high-quality semisweet chocolate, broken into small pieces

1 tbsp. vanilla extract

8 tbsp. unsalted butter, cut into small pieces and brought to room temperature

1 baked 9-inch graham cracker pie shell

Optional: fresh raspberries or strawberries for garnish

Directions

Using a handheld electric mixer, whip 1 cup cream into stiff peaks in a medium bowl, adding powdered sugar as it gets firm. Refrigerate.

Meanwhile, combine eggs, sugar, salt, and water in double boiler or deep, heat-tolerant bowl set over an inch of barely simmering—not boiling—water. Use a handheld electric mixer to beat mixture for 5 minutes, until it's glossy and somewhat thickened. Turn burner to lowest setting.

Stir in chocolate pieces and vanilla until chocolate is melted and mixture is fully combined. Remove mixture from heat. Cool to room temperature, placing pan over a bowl of ice water if desired, to hasten process.

Beat in butter pieces until mixture is smooth. Fold in whipped cream reserved for filling, until evenly combined. Spoon filling into baked and cooled pie shell. Refrigerate until set, about three hours.

Top with remaining cream, whipped to soft peaks, and fresh berries, if desired.

Maple-Walnut Tart

Makes a 10-inch tart, or a deep-dish 9-inch pie

Walnuts are a good source of Omega-3s (for brain function), protein, copper, magnesium, and vitamins B6 and E. They have antioxidant and anti-inflammatory benefits that protect against cardiovascular disease as well as type 2 diabetes. They also lower the risk of certain cancers, including prostate cancer and breast cancer.

Can also be made with pecans, pine nuts, or other nuts. The pecan version makes a pecan pie similar to the one so loved in the South, but with more maple flavor—and no corn syrup, which saves a little pantry space.

Ingredients

8 oz. (2 cups) coarsely chopped walnuts, pecans, or pine nuts

1 prepared deep-dish 9-inch pie or 10-inch tart shell, unbaked

3 large eggs

2 tsp. vanilla extract

1 cup maple syrup

½ cup granulated sugar

6 tbsp. unsalted butter

1 tsp. kosher salt

Directions

Preheat oven to 325 degrees. Roast walnuts 6–8 minutes, until fragrant and toasted. Remove from oven; increase oven temperature to 375. Pierce pie shell all over with tines of a fork. Line with foil and fill with pie weights if available. Line the outside with heavy foil to collect any leaks or drips. Bake 12 minutes. Remove from oven. Remove interior foil and weights. Fill tart shell with toasted walnuts; set aside.

Meanwhile, in a medium bowl, whisk together eggs and vanilla extract. Set aside. In a 2–quart saucepan, combine maple syrup, sugar, butter, and salt. Cook over medium heat, stirring constantly, until mixture reaches a boil. Boil 1 minute, stirring constantly. Remove from heat. Temper the mixture: slowly pour ¼ cup filling into eggs, whisking vigorously. Repeat with another ¼ cup. Whisk egg mixture into filling.

Carefully ladle filling over walnuts, leaving ¼–½ inch space below rim. Bake tart at 375 degrees until just set in the center, about 30 minutes, and checking after 20 minutes. If crust is golden-brown before the filling is set, cover edges loosely with foil or pie shield.

Streusel-Topped Raspberry, Lemon, or Apricot Bars

Makes 24–36 bars

This easy recipe is attractive and simple, and it will be popular if you're feeding a crowd. I like the flexibility of using your favorite fruit preserves and the taste of the crust, which resembles shortbread.

Ingredients

2½ cups all-purpose flour
1 cup sugar
1 tsp. salt
1 tsp. dried ginger or ½ tsp. freshly grated nutmeg
¼ cup heavy cream or sour cream

1 cup (2 sticks) cold butter, each one cut into 8–10 pieces
1 cup finely chopped walnuts or pecans (or slivered almonds)
16 oz. fruit preserves, such as raspberry or apricot (or lemon curd)

Directions

Combine first 4 ingredients in a food processor. Pulse several times. Add cream; pulse about 10 times. Add butter in two batches, then nuts. Pulse only until mix has formed pea-sized clumps, but is still crumbly. Remove about ¾ cup for topping; process remaining dough several more pulses, until it starts to form one or two masses.

Coat a 13x9x2 pan with nonstick spray. Dump larger portion of dough into pan; press down firmly. Top with jam. Sprinkle with reserved dough crumbles.

Bake at 350 degrees for 35–40 minutes, until golden. Cool completely; cut into squares.

For lemon version, refrigerate after bringing to room temperature.

9 Lives of Brownies
Makes 24–48 brownies

I used to wonder why people bothered with homemade brownies. I thought store-bought mix was pretty good. Still, I was never able to bake the prefab version without a bunch of moist brownie ending up on the cutting knife. Besides that, I'm interested in flavor variations. On a lark, I included marshmallow crème in my recipe and created a fudgy texture that's easy to cut into pieces.

Darker, lower-sugar chocolate like semisweet can lower blood pressure, and it can even decrease cholesterol levels, lowering the possibility of heart disease. It may also help reduce the symptoms of migraines, protect against dementia, and raise serotonin levels, which can alleviate depression. Semisweet chocolate also contains a good amount of iron.

Fudgy Brownies and Basic Directions

In a medium saucepan over low heat, combine 2 cups semisweet chocolate chips, 1 stick (4 oz.) butter, 1 tsp. kosher salt, and 1 cup packed light brown sugar. Cook, stirring often, until sugar and butter melt. Turn off heat. Stir in 1 cup marshmallow crème until well combined; cool slightly. Whisk in 3 large eggs, one at a time, and 2 tsp. vanilla. Stir in 1 cup all-purpose flour. Spread in a greased 13x9x2 pan; bake at 325 degrees 45 minutes.

Walnut Brownies

Make Fudgy Brownies, folding in 1 cup chopped walnuts.

Peppermint Brownies

Make Fudgy Brownies. While warm, spread with peppermint icing, then sprinkle with crushed peppermints. For peppermint icing, place 6 tbsp. butter and ¼ cup heavy cream in a heavy saucepan. Heat on low until butter melts, whisking often. Add 20 Starlight mints, crushed, and 6 oz. cream cheese. Whisk constantly, still on low heat, until peppermints melt. Remove from heat; whisk in 2 cups powdered sugar. Peppermint sprinkle: crush, then sprinkle 10–12 Starlight mints on top.

Have extra peppermints on hand? Next time you want to brew tea, throw one or two per serving into very hot water as you brew the tea. Serve hot or iced.

Cheesecake Brownies

Make Fudgy Brownies. Spread in greased pan. Beat 4 oz. softened cream cheese, ¼ cup sugar, 1 egg, and 1 teaspoon vanilla. Swirl into brownie batter. Bake 45–55 minutes.

Peanut Butter or Almond Butter Brownies

Make Fudgy Brownies, folding in 1 cup chopped peanuts or almonds. Spread in prepared pan; swirl in ½ cup creamy peanut butter or almond butter before baking. If almond butter is too thick, heat in microwave on medium power for about a minute.

Tropical Brownies

Make Fudgy Brownies, folding in 1 cup chopped macadamia nuts. For the frosting, beat 2 sticks room-temperature butter, ¼ cup milk or cream, 2 tsp. vanilla, and 3 cups powdered sugar. Spread onto cooled brownies. Top with 1½ cups toasted flaked coconut.

Toffee Brownies

Make Fudgy Brownies, folding 1 cup toffee bits (such as Heath "Bits O' Brickle") into the batter. Top with ½ cup toffee bits before baking. Optional: frost with caramel glaze (separate recipe).

Raspberry Brownies

Make Fudgy Brownies. After pouring into baking dish, top with 18 oz. raspberry preserves that you've heated to drizzling consistency. Swirl into batter before baking. Dust cooled brownies with powdered sugar.

Butterscotch Blondies

Melt 1 stick butter in a heavy saucepan over low heat. Turn off heat; whisk in 1 cup marshmallow crème and 1 cup lightly packed light brown sugar. Whisk in 3 large eggs, 2 tbsp. bourbon or Amaretto (optional)—or 2 tbsp. water—and 2 tsp. vanilla.

Stir in 1 cup all-purpose flour, 1 tsp. Kosher salt, and 1 cup quick-cooking oats. Fold in 12 oz. butterscotch chips and ½ cup chopped nuts (optional). Bake in a generously greased and floured pan at 325 degrees 40–45 minutes. Optional: top with caramel glaze (separate recipe).

Bread Pudding

12–16 servings

Did you know that in thirteenth century England, bread pudding was known as "poor man's pudding," a popular way for the lower classes to use stale bread? It's still good for that, but it's also come a long way!

Add your own favorite flavors. Some of my favorites are listed below. In addition to traditional bourbon sauce, try caramel or curacao sauces (separate recipes). Try making individual muffin-size puddings (see below).

Ingredients

1 lb. baguette, or similar bread, torn into bite-sized pieces (slightly stale is fine)

Optional: 1 cup chopped nuts such as walnuts, pecans, or pine nuts

6 large eggs

2 12-oz. cans evaporated milk

1½ cups granulated sugar

1 tbsp. vanilla extract

2 tsp. ground cinnamon or nutmeg

Juice and zest of 1 medium "juice" orange, such as Valencia (about ½ cup)

1 tsp. kosher salt

8 tbsp. (1 stick) butter

Optional: 1 large or 2 small apples, peeled, cored, and chopped

Optional: ½ cup raisins or Craisins

Directions

Preheat oven to 325 degrees. Toast baguette pieces until very dry and just starting to brown, 6–8 minutes. Remove from oven; leave oven on. If using nuts, put them in oven until toasted, about 5 minutes. Coat a 13x9x2 pan with nonstick spray (or use standard muffin pans or mini muffin pans).

In a large bowl, beat eggs. Whisk in milk, sugar, vanilla, cinnamon, orange juice, zest, and salt; add bread and stir well. Let stand 10 minutes.

In a medium saucepan, melt butter over medium-low heat. Add apples and raisins/craisins. Sauté 5 minutes, until berries are plump and apples are starting to soften. Stir fruit mixture and toasted nuts into bread mixture. Pour into prepared dish. If not using fruit and nuts, stir melted butter into bread mixture.

Bake until set and starting to brown, 45–60 minutes, covering during first 30 minutes. If using standard muffin pans, bake for 25 minutes. For mini muffin pans, bake for 15 minutes. Serve warm, with your choice of sauces.

Bourbon Sauce (Traditional) Ingredients

1 stick unsalted butter
1 cup granulated sugar
½ cup whipping cream

¼ cup bourbon, brandy, or cognac
Pinch of kosher salt

Directions

Melt butter in heavy saucepan over medium heat. Whisk in remaining ingredients. Simmer until thickened, whisking often, about 3 minutes.

Mexican Bread Pudding

Use pecans or pine nuts. Use dark brown sugar, lightly packed, instead of granulated. For spice, use cinnamon. Top with caramel sauce (separate recipe).

Pumpkin Bread Pudding

Use pecans. For liquid, use 1 can evaporated milk and 1 can pumpkin puree. For sugar, use light brown sugar, lightly packed, instead of granulated sugar. For spices, use 1 tsp. each cinnamon, nutmeg, and ginger. Top with caramel sauce.

Orange-Blueberry Bread Pudding

Eliminate raisins/craisins. Add nuts to bread mixture, and then place in baking pan. Sprinkle with about 2 cups of blueberries. Sprinkle with ¼ cup granulated sugar. Bake, covered with foil, about 50 minutes. Top with Curacao sauce (separate recipe).

Lemon Trifle

8 generous servings

This can be served in a large footed glass bowl, which is a traditional British presentation, or in wine glasses. Try different types of cake. I like angel food as well as traditional pound cake. For a variation, substitute blueberry sauce (separate recipe) for the fresh berries.

Shortcut: substitute prepared lemon pudding from a store-bought mix for the curd mixture.

Ingredients

2 cups prepared lemon curd (store bought or separate recipe)

1 12-oz. can evaporated milk

1 store-bought pound cake or half an angel food cake

2 pints fresh blueberries or blackberries

2 cups whipped topping such as whipped cream

Optional: about ¼ cup slivered toasted almonds for garnish

Optional: about ⅓ cup fruity liqueur such as limoncello or Grand Marnier (for garnish)

Directions

Stir milk into curd. Set aside. Cut cake into bite-sized cubes. Rinse and drain berries.

Make layers: Cake, limoncello, curd mixture, berries, and cream. Repeat. Top with berries and garnish with nuts and liqueur if desired.

Buttermilk Cookies with Cream Cheese Frosting

Makes about 60 individual small cookies (or 30 sandwich cookies)

For a quick filling, in lieu of frosting, consider using store-bought preserves, such as raspberry. You can also add about ¼ cup of preserves to the frosting below for a tasty combination. I like to think of these sandwich cookies as "poor man's macarons," after the fancy French cookies (different from our coconut macaroons).

Cookies

½ cup (1 stick) butter, softened
1 cup granulated sugar
1 large egg
2 tsp. vanilla extract
2½ cups all-purpose flour
½ tsp. ground nutmeg

Optional ingredients: ½ tsp. cardamom, 1 tsp. lemon zest
½ tsp. baking soda
½ tsp. salt
½ cup buttermilk

Frosting

4 tbsp. softened butter
3 oz. softened cream cheese

1½ cups powdered sugar
1 tsp. vanilla extract

Directions

For cookies, preheat oven to 375 degrees. Using an electric mixer, cream butter and sugar. Add egg and vanilla; beat well.

Whisk together next 5 ingredients. Gradually add to creamed mixture, alternating with buttermilk, until well mixed. Scoop using a small spoon. Drop onto parchment-lined cookie sheets, leaving at least an inch between cookies. Bake at 375 for 10–12 minutes until lightly browned. Cool before frosting. You may either frost the tops of cookies or make into sandwich cookies.

For frosting, beat together butter, cream cheese, powdered sugar, and vanilla until smooth.

Italian Cream Cake Option

Add ¾ cup coconut to batter, along with ¾ cup chopped toasted nuts such as walnuts. To frosting, add another ¼ cup coconut and ¼ cup chopped nuts. After frosting the cookies, add another ¼ cup coconut if desired.

Red Velvet Option

Add 3 tbsp. cocoa to batter and eliminate spices and zest. Add ½ tsp. red food coloring if desired. Optional: top frosted cookies with coconut.

Double Chocolate Peppermint Sandwich Cookies

Add ½ cup cocoa to batter. Eliminate spices and zest. Stir in 6 oz. semisweet chocolate chips to mixed batter. Top with peppermint icing (see brownie recipe).

Double Chocolate Nut Butter Sandwich Cookies

Make double chocolate dough. Make filling by mixing ½ cup nut butter—such as peanut, almond, or hazelnut—1 cup powdered sugar, and 3 tbsp. buttermilk or regular milk.

Orange Cream Option

See separate recipe.

Sauces, Pestos, and Preserves

Apricot Pepper Preserves

Makes about 6 half-pint jars

Serving Ideas

Good with turkey burgers, ham and cheese sandwiches, turkey sandwiches, pork, chicken, fish, crab cakes, and over Brie cheese. Great idea for a hostess gift!

Peppadew peppers were originally discovered in South Africa. Cherry tomato-sized, they are often available hulled, seeded, and pickled in brine. They have a little heat but have enough natural sweetness to balance the burn.

Ingredients

2 cups chopped dried apricots (about 12 oz.) soaked in ¾ cup apple cider vinegar for at least an hour

1 cup minced jalapeno pepper

⅔ cup minced red bell pepper (can be roasted peppers from a jar)

⅓ cup minced peppadew peppers (from a jar or the salad bar at well-stocked groceries)

¼ cup peppadew liquid

24 oz. mango, peach or apricot nectar

½ cup sugar—more to taste

3 tbsp. "no sugar needed" powdered pectin, such as Ball brand

Directions

Combine all ingredients except pectin in a heavy saucepan. Bring to a rolling boil over medium-high heat, stirring often. Boil for 2 minutes. Reduce heat to medium, add pectin, and simmer, stirring often, 2 minutes. Reduce heat to low and cook for 10 minutes, to allow flavors to combine. Fill sterilized jars and seal tightly.

If the peppers rise to the top of each jar, you may want to turn them over shortly after filling for an hour, then turn right side up to distribute peppers evenly.

To sterilize jars, submerge canning jars in a stock pot full of simmering water for at least 5 minutes. I place a silicone hot pad in the bottom of the pan to keep jars from clanking and to prevent any chance of a jar breaking.

Avocado Spread

Makes 1–1½ cups

Avocados are a top antioxidant food with good amounts of vitamins A and C, potassium, magnesium, fiber, and cholesterol-fighting power.

One thing I like about this spread is that it doesn't turn brown for many hours—more than twenty-four hours in my experience. I think it's the yogurt.

Serving Ideas

For sandwiches, such as roasted vegetable or turkey and Swiss, or on burgers.

Ingredients

1 large or 2 small avocados
1 tbsp. lime juice or lemon juice
1 tbsp. plain Greek yogurt

Garlic salt and/or onion salt to taste
Black pepper to taste
Optional: dash hot sauce

Directions

Combine all ingredients with a fork. Chill until ready to use.

Bechamel Sauce

Makes about 2½ cups

See separate recipes for incorporating in Chicken Mornay, asparagus or green bean gratin. The option for adding goat cheese is not traditional, but it gives the recipe a little extra personality.

Ingredients

6 tbsp. unsalted butter

⅓ cup flour

4 cups whole milk (you can use 2 12-oz. cans of evaporated milk, plus enough water to make 4 cups diluted)

⅓ cup dry white wine

1 tsp. kosher salt

½ tsp. white or black pepper

1 bay leaf

1 tsp. thyme (or nutmeg for cheesy sauces)

Optional: for a little tang, add 4 oz. goat cheese

Directions

Melt butter in a saucepan over medium heat. Add flour and cook, whisking constantly, about 2 minutes. Do not brown. Whisk in milk, bay leaf, wine, thyme, and salt. Bring just to a boil, stirring often to prevent burning. Reduce heat to low and simmer 10 minutes, stirring every few minutes.

Remove bay leaf. If sauce is too thick, add chicken broth, vegetable broth, wine, or milk. If adding cheese, add at end, just after turning off heat. Stir until melted.

Chili Lime Sauce

Makes about ½ cup

Serving Ideas

Serve with fried green tomatoes, cornmeal-crusted tilapia, or Tex-Mex seafood dishes, such as fish tacos.

Ingredients

½ cup mayonnaise—regular or light

2 tbsp. lime juice

1 tsp. chili powder

½ tsp. garlic powder

Optional: dash hot sauce, salt, sugar

Directions

Whisk together first four ingredients. Add optional ingredients to taste.

Chimichurri Sauce

Makes about 1 cup

This steak sauce is traditionally served with flank steak (as in Argentina). It's also good with burgers, grilled white-flesh fish, salmon, and pan-fried tilapia (separate recipes).

Parsley is a good source of vitamins C and K. It promotes heart health and helps fight breast cancer and arthritis. It's part of the carrot family.

Ingredients

3 cups, packed, flat-leaf parsley leaves with tender stems (about 1 large bunch)

1 medium shallot, peeled and quartered

5 garlic cloves, peeled

⅓ cup olive oil

1 tbsp. red wine vinegar

2 tbsp. lemon or lime juice—more to taste

Optional: up to 1 tbsp. coriander or cilantro chutney* (or ½ cup chopped cilantro)

Optional, for creamier version: add 1 avocado, peeled and mashed

Salt and black pepper to taste: start with about ½ tsp. of each

Directions

Wash parsley; drain well. Combine all ingredients in a food processor. Process until well blended. Chill until ready to use.

*Such as Swad brand coriander chutney (or see separate recipe for cilantro chutney)

Cilantro Chutney

Makes about ½ cup

Serving Ideas

This is a key ingredient in pepita pesto; also use in chimichurri sauce, green salsa, and other Tex-Mex foods, couscous cakes, and bean burgers (separate recipes). Add to ranch dressing for a Southwestern accent. For Indian dishes, stir into plain yogurt (similar to raita). Use your imagination!

Cilantro is rich in antioxidants, essential oils, vitamins, and dietary fiber, which help reduce LDL (bad cholesterol) while increasing HDL (good cholesterol) levels. It's also rich in vitamins A, C, and K.

Ingredients

3 cups packed cilantro leaves along with tender stems (about 2 oz.) washed and dried thoroughly

3 tbsp. red wine vinegar

3 tbsp. olive or vegetable oil

6 cloves garlic, peeled

½–1 tsp. ground cumin, to taste

Dash hot sauce

Salt and pepper to taste

Dash sugar, if mixture tastes sour or bitter

Directions

Puree all in food processor. Adjust seasonings.

Hollandaise, Béarnaise, and Aioli Sauces

Makes about ¾ cup

Hollandaise Sauce

Serving Ideas

Serve over baked or poached eggs, steamed broccoli, asparagus, or green beans. Try with cornmeal-crusted tilapia or crab cakes.

Ingredients

4 large egg yolks

1 tbsp. lemon juice

Optional: 1 tsp. lemon zest

1 stick butter (8 tbsp.)—regular or light—cut into bits

Pinch smoked paprika or cayenne

Pinch salt, if needed

Directions

Vigorously whisk egg yolks and lemon juice in top of heat tolerant glass or metal bowl for 90 seconds, to thicken and increase volume somewhat. Add zest. Place over a close-fitting saucepan containing simmering water, set over medium low heat. Water should not touch bottom of bowl.

Add butter in several batches, stirring often as it melts. Once butter has melted, whisk by hand 2–3 minutes, until sauce is somewhat thickened and has doubled in volume. Or use whip attachment of an electric mixer. Sauce will thicken further upon standing. Remove from heat, whisk in cayenne and salt. If sauce gets too thick, whisk in 1–2 tbsp. warm water before serving.

For roasted pepper hollandaise, add ⅓ cup minced roasted red bell peppers at the end of the directions above, combining with a hand immersion blender if desired.

Béarnaise Sauce

Serving Ideas

Serve with steak, other grilled beef, steamed broccoli, or poached eggs.

Directions

Follow recipe for hollandaise, but add 1tsp. dried tarragon, 1 tbsp. wine vinegar, and 1 minced shallot.

Shortcut Aioli

Serving Ideas

Serve with fish, roasted potatoes, or sandwiches.

Directions

Follow recipe for hollandaise. Add ⅓ cup vegetable oil, 3 tbsp. olive oil, and 2 cloves minced garlic.

Spicy Aioli

This works great for fish tacos, crab cakes, or fried green tomatoes. Add 1–2 tbsp. hot sauce (such as Sriracha) and 1–2 tbsp. lemon or lime juice.

Lemon Butter Sauce with Almonds

Makes 1 generous cup

Serving Ideas

Pasta: Toss with fettuccine. Add steamed veggies if desired; sprinkle with garlic salt. **Vegetables:** Serve over steamed broccoli (with or without almonds), steamed green beans, or asparagus (with almonds). Try tossing with spaghetti squash and top with almonds. See roasted potato recipe below.

Ingredients

4 tbsp. butter—regular or light

2 tbsp. lemon juice

2 tsp. lemon zest

8 oz. chicken or vegetable broth

Optional: ¼ cup slivered almonds, toasted

Salt and pepper to taste

Directions

Melt butter in saucepan over medium heat. Add lemon juice, zest, and broth. Bring to a boil; lower heat slightly and cook until somewhat thickened, stirring occasionally, about 5 minutes. Add optional almonds, salt, and pepper to taste.

Lemon Butter Roasted Potatoes

Ingredients

2 lb. red or Yukon gold potatoes

Lemon butter sauce ingredients (above) doubled (excluding almonds)

Optional: 1 tbsp. dried rosemary

Optional: 1 cup grated Parmesan cheese

Preheat oven to 425 degrees. Peel potatoes if desired; cut into large bite-sized pieces and place in saucepan. Follow directions for lemon butter sauce through bringing to a boil. Pour sauce over potatoes.

Bring to a boil over medium heat; boil uncovered, stirring often, until liquid is greatly reduced, about 12 minutes. Pour potato mixture into roasting pan. Sprinkle with salt and pepper to taste. Roast until tender and beginning to brown, 25–30 minutes, sprinkling with cheese after 10 minutes if desired.

Master Pesto Recipes

Serving Ideas

See individual recipe ideas below. Dollop onto soups, toss with pasta, stir into rice (or vegetables such as white potatoes or green beans), use as a sandwich spread, stir into scrambled eggs, or spread on pizza. Use your imagination! Undecided? Try on a cracker—with a glass of wine—while you ponder.

With some fresh greens, you may feel like you've just processed lawn clippings. In that case, just add oil and cheese until you feel like you've rejoined the culinary world.

Green Leafy Pestos: Arugula, Basil, Kale, Mustard/Turnip/Collard Greens
Makes about 1½ cups

Ingredients

5 cloves fresh garlic
½ cup chopped almonds, walnuts, pecans, pine nuts, hazelnuts, or pistachios (toasted)
¼ cup extra virgin olive oil—more to taste
2 oz. Parmesan cheese, grated (or try another white cheese such as Fontina, Feta, or cotija)
About 5 cups rinsed greens (coarsely chopped and packed)

Lemon juice to taste—up to 2 tbsp.
Optional : 1–2 tbsp. capers with their brine to add saltiness and slight bitterness (works well with greens that are relatively mild, such as collard greens)
Salt and pepper to taste

Pulse all ingredients in a food processor until well combined. Add more olive oil, salt, pepper, and lemon juice to taste.

Broccoli Pesto

Makes about 2 cups

Serving Ideas

Try adding to cooked rice in a ratio of 2 parts rice to 1 part broccoli pesto. Top with grated Parmesan cheese.

Ingredients

10 oz. broccoli florets

⅓ cup olive oil

½ cup finely grated Parmesan cheese

¼ cup toasted nuts

3 cloves garlic, peeled

1 tbsp. lemon juice

Salt and pepper to taste

Optional: hot sauce to taste

Combine all in food processor. Pulse until mixture reaches desired consistency.

Sun-Dried Tomato Pesto

Makes about 1 cup

Serving Ideas

Use as a topping, with goat cheese, over crackers, or for a fried eggplant appetizer.

Ingredients

1 cup sun-dried tomatoes in olive oil, drained, from a jar

3 tbsp. oil from the jar

3 garlic cloves, peeled

Optional: ¼ cup fresh basil leaves (or 1 tsp. dried basil)

½ cup finely grated Parmesan cheese

Optional: 2–3 tbsp. fine breadcrumbs, for thickening

Combine all in food processor.

Roasted Red Bell Pepper Pesto

Makes about 1 cup

Serving Ideas

Serve with flank steak, crab cakes, or fish. Layer into tortas, in overnight rolls, or with corn cakes.

Ingredients

2 roasted red bell peppers from a jar (about 8 oz.)

2 tbsp. olive oil

¼ cup toasted slivered almonds, walnuts, pistachios, or pine nuts

½ cup finely grated Parmesan cheese (about 1 oz.) or use 2 oz. crumbled cotija or Feta cheese

2 cloves fresh garlic

2 tsp. red wine vinegar

Salt and black pepper to taste

Combine all in food processor.

Artichoke Pesto

Makes about 2 cups

Serving Ideas

Serve with pasta, crackers, or bruschetta. Use as tart filling (fill baked shells with pesto, top with chopped nuts and a bit of cayenne pepper for color). Or try on a ham sandwich.

Ingredients

1–14 oz. can quartered artichoke hearts, drained and rinsed

3 tbsp. olive oil (more to taste)

⅓ cup roasted walnuts or pine nuts (more for topping if desired)

3 oz. goat cheese

Salt and pepper to taste

Mix all in food processor.

Pumpkin Seed (Pepita) Pesto

Makes about 1 cup

Serving Ideas

Try a dollop on soups such as Portuguese white bean, butternut squash, red pepper tomato, or potato leek. Also try on your favorite green salad (instead of croutons).

Pepitas are a good source of fiber, protein, and several minerals. They have been shown to have a positive effect on the production of mood-enhancing serotonin.

Ingredients

1 cup roasted and salted pepitas

¼ cup olive oil—more to taste

5 cloves fresh garlic, peeled

½ cup finely grated Parmesan cheese or other hard cheese such as cotija (for a more crumbly texture)

2 tbsp. coriander chutney (such as Swad brand), homemade cilantro chutney, or ¾ cup chopped cilantro

Black pepper to taste

Combine all in small food processor.

Pomegranate Pepper Preserves

Makes about 6 8-oz. jars

Pomegranates are a good source of vitamin C and potassium, which may help lower cholesterol. Jalapenos are a good source of vitamin B6, vitamin C, and capsaicin, which has bacterial-, cholesterol-, and diabetes-fighting powers.

Serving Ideas

Try with turkey burgers, ham, or turkey and cheese sandwiches. Try with roasted turkey at Thanksgiving (instead of cranberry sauce), or with Greek or Swedish meatballs (see separate recipe for Greek meatballs).

Ingredients

1½ cup minced jalapeno peppers

1½ cup minced red bell pepper (roasted, from a jar, are okay)

⅓ cup minced peppadew peppers

¼ cup peppadew liquid

16 oz. pomegranate juice

1¼ cup fruity white wine (such as Riesling)

⅔ cup red wine vinegar

¾ cup sugar—to taste

3 tbsp. "no sugar needed" powdered pectin (such as Ball brand)

Directions

Combine all ingredients except pectin in a heavy saucepan. Heat over medium-high heat until mixture boils, stirring often. Reduce heat to medium, add pectin, and simmer, stirring often, 2 minutes. Reduce heat to low and cook for 15 minutes, to allow flavors to combine.

Fill sterilized jars and seal tightly. If peppers rise to top of each jar, you can turn them over shortly after filling for about an hour, then turn right side up to distribute peppers evenly.

Pomegranate Sauce

Makes 1–1½ cups (enough for at least 1 lb. of pork tenderloin, salmon fillets, or chicken)

Ingredients

1 tbsp. olive oil

2 tbsp. minced shallots

1 tsp. dried rosemary, crushed to release flavor

1 cup pomegranate juice

3 tbsp. maple syrup or honey

2 tbsp. red wine vinegar

Optional: ¼ cup hearty red wine

Optional: ½ cup dried cherries or cranberries

1 tbsp. butter

Directions

Heat a small saucepan over medium heat. Add ingredients through red wine; bring to a boil, stirring often. Reduce heat to medium-low. Add optional fruit. Simmer until reduced by a third, about 20 minutes, stirring occasionally. Remove from heat; stir in butter. For a thicker, smoother consistency, blend with an immersion blender.

Remoulade Sauce

Makes about 1¼ cups sauce

Serving Ideas

Serve with crab or salmon cakes, fish or shrimp tacos, or fried green tomatoes.

Originally from France, remoulade sauce has been adapted by the Cajun culture of southeastern Louisiana. It is a variation of mayonnaise, which has both Spanish and French roots. Mayonnaise was first used in the Spanish town of Mahon, but it was popularized by the French (whose navy captured the Port of Mahon during the Seven Years War in 1756). Some Francophiles contend the name comes from the old French word "moyeu" which means egg yolk.

Ingredients

1 cup mayonnaise—regular or light

1 tbsp. lemon juice

3 tbsp. pickles such as bread and butter, minced

1½ tbsp. capers, minced

1 tbsp. chopped parsley leaves

1 tsp. anchovy paste or fish sauce

½ tsp. Worcestershire sauce

2 tbsp. ketchup

Optional (for spicy version): ¼–½ tsp. cayenne pepper (or use black pepper)

Directions

Combine all ingredients in food processor; pulse a few times for them to blend. Refrigerate at least 30 minutes before serving.

Summer Tomato Jam

Makes 2 cups

Serving Ideas

Serve on a BLT, grilled cheese, roasted veggie, or turkey and Brie sandwich. Try with avocado if you like. It complements goat cheese, tapenade, and pesto flavors. For convenience, look for tubes of grated ginger in the fresh produce section of your grocery.

Tomatoes are a good source of Vitamin A, Vitamin C, and potassium. Lycopene, especially from cooked tomatoes, has shown cancer-fighting properties. This jam is a beautiful, glossy bright red color, especially when made with grape tomatoes. Citrus zests are high in fiber and flavonoids, which fight cancer and diabetes and lower cholesterol.

Ingredients

1½ lb. Roma tomatoes, including pulp, cored and chopped coarsely (or use halved grape tomatoes)
1 shallot, minced
2 tsp. lemon zest
3 tbsp. fresh lemon juice
Optional: 1 tbsp. cognac or brandy

1 tbsp. peeled grated ginger
½ cup granulated sugar
½ tsp. ground cumin
¼ tsp. black pepper
¼ tsp. red pepper flakes
1 tsp. kosher salt

Directions

Combine all ingredients in a medium-sized heavy saucepan. Cook over medium heat, stirring often, until mixture boils. Reduce heat to medium-low and gently simmer, uncovered, stirring occasionally, until mixture is thick and syrupy, 30–40 minutes. Cool; season with salt and pepper. Store in refrigerator.

Kalamata Olive Tapenade

Makes 1 generous cup

Serving Ideas

Layer into mini cheese tortas or with pestos (separate recipes). Serve over goat cheese or on crackers (with a dollop of tomato jam if desired). Use as a sandwich spread for tuna salad or ham and cheese. Serve on Irish brown bread or pumpernickel cocktail bread, with smoked salmon and cream cheese. Serve over oven-roasted asparagus.

   For a special treat, try a smoked salmon BLT sandwich. Add a layer of tapenade to a sandwich made from layers of smoked salmon, cream or goat cheese, bacon, lettuce, and tomato.

Ingredients

6–7 oz. jar pitted Kalamata olives, drained
1 tsp. capers in brine, drained
½ tsp. anchovy paste or fish sauce
2 tsp. red wine vinegar
1 tbsp. olive oil

3 cloves garlic, peeled
½ a medium red onion, cut into several chunks
   (or use 2 shallots)
Freshly ground black pepper to taste

Directions

Pulse all in a food processor till mixture reaches desired consistency.

Blueberry Sauce

Makes about 1½ cups sauce

Use as a topping for cheesecake or vanilla ice cream, or incorporate in a lemon trifle (separate recipe). Try as a pancake topping. See ideas below for using as a savory sauce for salmon, pork, or roasted turkey.

Blueberries are rich in nutrients. Studies have shown they may improve memory. Since blueberries may delay Alzheimer's disease, they've been nicknamed the "brain berry." They are a top antioxidant food and have good amounts of vitamin C and fiber.

 Native Americans called blueberries "star fruits." They put them in honey pudding and used them in dried meat pies. And they shared these early energy bars with Lewis and Clark!

Ingredients

1 lb. blueberries, rinsed and picked over (or use frozen)

1½ tbsp. fresh lemon juice

2 tbsp. butter—regular or light

1½ tbsp. minced crystallized ginger or ginger marmalade (or 2 tsp. ground ginger)

¼ cup granulated sugar (for savory applications, use 1–2 tbsp. to taste)

½ tsp. ground cardamom or nutmeg (for savory dishes, use 1–2 tsp. of your favorite herb, such as dried rosemary, crushed)

Optional, for thickening: 1 tbsp. flour

Up to 1 tsp. kosher salt (to taste)

Directions

Combine ingredients through cardamom in a heavy saucepan. Heat over medium heat until mixture boils. Stir in flour and salt. Reduce heat to medium-low and cook 5 minutes.

Caramel Sauce

About 1½ cups sauce

Serving Ideas

Serve over Mexican bread pudding, vanilla ice cream, or cheesecake. It is also tasty with apple and pear desserts.

Ingredients

1 stick (8 tbsp.) unsalted butter

1¼ cups packed dark brown sugar*

½ cup heavy cream

½ tsp. kosher salt

Directions

In a heavy saucepan over medium-low heat, melt butter. Whisk in brown sugar until well combined. Whisk in cream and salt; stir until sugar dissolves and sauce is bubbly, about 3 minutes.

*To make a caramel glaze that hardens (such as to coat sweet rolls, brownies, or cookies), reduce brown sugar to 1 cup and whisk in 1 cup sifted powdered sugar after cooling the mixture for several minutes. Use an electric mixer if necessary to remove any clumps of powdered sugar.

Curacao Sauce

Makes about ¾ cup sauce

Serving Ideas

Serve with blueberry bread pudding, ricotta cake, or ice cream.

Ingredients

1 stick (8 tbsp.) unsalted butter
1 cup granulated sugar
½ cup whipping cream

¼ cup Curacao or similar orange-flavored liqueur
Pinch kosher salt

Directions

Melt butter in heavy saucepan over medium heat. Whisk in remaining ingredients. Bring to a boil, reduce heat to medium-low, and simmer 5 minutes.

Lemon, Lime, or Orange Curd

Makes about 1 pint (curd freezes well, in canning jars, for up to a year)

Thanks to my friend Phyllis for inventing the pie filling by adding condensed milk! See pie recipes (below) for lemon icebox pie and key lime pie. See also separate recipes for incorporating curd into lemon trifle. Try a dollop on cheesecake, or use as a filling for gingersnap sandwich cookies.

Ingredients

¾ cup fresh lemon juice, from 6–8 lemons (Meyer lemons are the best, if you can find them!)

2 tbsp. cornstarch

Optional: 1 tbsp. finely grated fresh lemon zest

¾ cup granulated sugar

1 stick (8 tbsp.) unsalted butter, cut into 8–10 pieces

½ tsp. salt

4 large egg yolks

Directions

In heavy saucepan, unheated, whisk cornstarch into lemon juice. Set heat to medium; cook lemon juice mixture, plus zest, sugar, butter, and salt, whisking often, 2 minutes, or until mixture begins to boil.

Lightly beat yolks in a small bowl. Drizzle in ¼ cup lemon mixture, whisking to temper eggs. Pour tempered yolk mixture into stovetop lemon mixture, whisking to combine. Bring to a boil; reduce heat to low and cook, whisking constantly, until curd is somewhat thickened, about 2 minutes. Cool and chill.

For lime curd, use lime juice (or Key lime juice) instead of lemon juice.

For orange curd, use ½ cup fresh orange juice and ¼ cup lime juice (reduce sugar to ½ cup).

Optional: add 1 tbsp. Curacao liqueur. Try with pumpkin-apple bread, separate recipe.

For lemon icebox pie or key lime pie, add 1 can sweetened condensed milk to 1 pint curd. Need more filling? Want to lighten a bit? Add 1 cup of plain Greek yogurt. Top with fresh fruit, such as blueberries or blueberry sauce (separate recipe), if desired.

Orange Cream

Makes about 2 cups

Serving Ideas

Try as a frosting for cake (such as carrot cake). Also good as a filling for gingersnap sandwich cookies.

Ingredients

4 oz. cream cheese, room temperature

2 tbsp. unsalted butter, room temperature

1 tsp. vanilla extract

2 tbsp. orange juice

½ tsp. ground ginger

2½ cups powdered sugar, plus more as needed

Dash salt

Optional: 1 tbsp. orange-flavored liqueur such as Curacao

2 tsp. grated orange zest

Directions

In a medium bowl, combine all ingredients except zest; mix until smooth, adding more powdered sugar as needed. Filling should have consistency of frosting. Stir in zest by hand, so it doesn't stick to beaters.

Orange-Vanilla Glaze

Serving Ideas

Try over scones, on peach or mango bread, or on overnight sweet rolls (separate recipes). Variation: if you want a plain vanilla glaze, substitute milk or cream for the orange juice, and eliminate zest.

Ingredients

1½ cups powdered sugar

3–4 tbsp. orange juice (more if needed for drizzling)

2 tsp. orange zest

1 tsp. vanilla extract

Optional (to taste): 1–2 tbsp. minced crystallized ginger (or ginger marmalade)

Directions

Put powdered sugar in a bowl. Mix orange juice, zest, and vanilla extract. Whisk into sugar to make a smooth glaze. Stir in optional ginger.

Index